LGBTQ
COMEDIC
MONOLOGUES
THAT ARE
ACTUALLY
FUNNY

Edited by

ALISHA GADDIS

APPLAUSE
THEATRE & CINEMA BOOKS
An Imprint of Hal Leonard Corporation

Published in 2016 by Applause Theatre & Cinema Books
An Imprint of Hal Leonard Corporation
7777 West Bluemound Road
Milwaukee, WI 53213

Trade Book Division Editorial Offices
33 Plymouth St., Montclair, NJ 07042

Printed in the United States of America

Book design by UB Communications

Library of Congress Cataloging-in-Publication Data

Names: Gaddis, Alisha, editor.
Title: LGBTQ comedic monologues that are actually funny / edited by
  Alisha Gaddis.
Description: Milwaukee, WI : Applause Theatre & Cinema Books, 2016.
Identifiers: LCCN 2016020332 | ISBN 9781495025150 (pbk.)
Subjects: LCSH: Monologues. | Acting—Auditions. | Sexual
  minorities—Drama. | Comedy sketches.
Classification: LCC PN2080 .L525 2016 | DDC 812/.0450817—dc23
LC record available at https://lccn.loc.gov/2016020332

www.applausebooks.com

Contents

Introduction

This book is for you. You who are holding it.

This book is for the LGBTQ actor, as well as those auditioning for LGBTQ roles. Roles that are funny and meaty and diverse and complex and wonderful—just like you.

This book was written by members of the LGBTQ community and its allies. Did you know this is the FIRST book ever of its kind? The VERY first book specifically for the LGBTQ actor in an LGBTQ role.

As I write this, I have just given birth to my daughter, Indiana Maven. She isn't even a month old yet. I look at her, and I want her to be exactly who she is. I want her to grow up in a world that is supportive and inclusive. A world where she feels loved just by being herself. I want her to know that she is always enough. Precisely as she is. (I also want her to be really, REALLY funny!)

This book came about because that should be the norm and not the exception.

So take this book. Be YOU! Take a monologue that is actually funny and DO IT! Be the actor that makes them laugh, books the part, and steals the show—being EXACTLY who you are.

Alisha Gaddis

Weeping Willows Never Cry

Alisha Gaddis

PAULINA, 28 to 45

PAULINA *is a lesbian park ranger—obsessed with her job and her woods. She spends all her time in the woods and does not want to interact with people, but must. She is serious, but tries to make awkward jokes. The pace of the monologue alters between drawn-out bits for emphasis, and then moving on swiftly.*

PAULINA   Watch your head—here comes the branch of Ulmus castaneifolia or chestnut-leafed elm for those of you who are not in the know.

Watch your head. Watch your head. Right this way.

My name is Paulina Bunyon, as my nametag reads. No, Paul Bunyon is not my twin brother—although some say I am built like an ox. [*Chuckles to herself.*]

Joking.

[*Clears throat.*] I am THE Park Ranger here at Kumquatanation National Park and Recreation Center. I started my training as an intern when I was a young twelve-year-old lass and have worked my way up the competitive park ranger ladder ever since. It was vicious and backstabbing as I am sure you are thinking—but worth the risks. You don't get this hat by just looking pretty. No siree.

Now, it is my duty to show you the grounds. Something I take seriously, because it is serious.

Some might say I OWN these woods. I say that. I say that a lot, actually.

This is my woods. My forest. My national land. I love my woods.

It may not bear my name, but we know each other. We get each other, intimately. By law it is yours, the people's, as well as mine. Not something I agree with, but my petitions have been denied by the county several times.

[*Looks off wistfully—sees boy by poisonous bush.*]

Hey, boy! Get away from that pretty berry bush—it may look ripe and delicious like a woman's loin, but it will eat you alive and leave you burning. Trust me. I've been there.

Okay. Where was I?

Let me point out that over to the left is the Gazebo of Dreams under the *Salix babylonica*—or weeping willow as you laymen all call it. Such a sad name. For a glorious creature. Some people love the gazebo—I love the tree. Look at her. Sheer beauty, grace, a quiet sadness. I only knew one girl like that. Leah Browning, seventh grade. I will never forget her silken hair shining in the sun like a *Salix babylonica* glistening in the morning dew. I wanted to hug her. I never did. But I hug THIS beauty all the time. And she always hugs back. No weeping here. Just hugs. Tree hugs.

Alright. As your park ranger and a park ranger to all—I must point out this creek. Look at all those families picnicking near. I wouldn't do that if I were you. This creek has excess fecal matter.

[*Beat.*]

No, tall man with baseball hat. Not human fecal matter. Don't be ridiculous. *Animal* fecal matter. For some reason animals love to shit in this creek. They excessively shit up Shit Creek and there is nothing we can do to stop it.

Let nature be nature.

Shit Creek is not a metaphor. It is real. It is natural. It is life.

And don't get too close while posing for your photos. You will get hand, foot, and mouth disease.

Okay. Over to your right you can see the Bridge of New Beginnings arching over Shit Creek. Some may call that ironic. I call it that. I call it that a lot.

Everyone seems to think THIS is a great place for pictures. If you choose to have your wedding here—you probably will too.

I am not married to anyone, because I am married to my job. Also, Sabrina said no when I asked her. But that was her mistake and not mine. Plus, she prefers birds over squirrels. Just from that—I should have known it would never work. Talk about a red flag.

I think the Bridge of New Beginnings it is a great place to watch the frolicking young *cervidaes*, or like the common idiot calls them—deer. I call them friends. I call them that a lot.

But they never call me. [*Chuckles to herself.*]

Joking.

[*Non-ironically.*] There is no cell reception down here.

So, this concludes the tour. I wish you all the best as husband and wife, husband and husband, etcetera and etcetera— mating is natural, after all. Just look at those rabbits humping.

And remember—if you have your special day here at Kumquatanation National Park and Recreation Center, please tell your guests to only leave footprints and take away memories.

Also, the porta-potties are over the hill on the right. Leave your shit where it belongs.

Breaking Bad News

Leah Mann

SAM, 40 to 45

SAM, *an androgynous woman, sits down in a well-appointed living room to break some devastating news to her beloved children.*

SAM   Okay, my darlings—please sit still and listen, because Mommy has something very important to tell you.

[*Beat.*]

It's been a long time coming and I'm sure you could tell that Mommy and Mommy have been fighting. You're not stupid, and I know even though we try to keep you two out of it, you can still feel the tension between us and I'm sorry for that.

[*Beat.*]

Sometimes mommies fall out of love. Sometimes one mommy is still in love and the other mommy starts acting distant so the first mommy gets frustrated and lashes out and then the mommies start fighting with each other and saying hurtful things. Then sometimes it turns out that the distant mommy was acting weird and cold because she started having an affair with another person, and not just any person, but a man that she works with who she's not even supposed to be sexually attracted to, but this cheating, lying mommy, has decided her sexuality is more tied up in intelligence and personality than gender or genitalia, despite making vows and having amazing sex with the mommy who never stopped being a supportive and loving partner.

[*Beat.*]

When your mom, Deenie, and I married, we merged our families into one, and that's not going to change.

Even though I adopted you, Rocco, and Deenie officially adopted you, Charlie, this split between us two mommies is not a split for you guys. We'll have joint custody. Half the time you'll stay here at the house with me, and the other half you'll stay with Mom Deenie and her new boyfriend at his loft where you can hear everything they do together and he can lead you in breathwork meditation. Apparently, he's also a wonderful cook—whose food I would enjoy if I were ever a big enough person to give him half a chance, so you'll eat well there.

Supposedly.

And sure, there's no yard for you to play in or parks nearby and all your friends are in this neighborhood, but it'll be a

growing experience for you guys and I'm sure you'll rise to
the occasion and not at all be traumatized by the cataclysmic
life change your other mommy is causing in all of our lives.

[*Beat.*]

Where is Mom Deenie, you might be wondering? Why am I
telling you this heartbreaking news all by myself? Good
question. If you see her maybe she'll tell you why she didn't
come home today when she promised that we would do this
together. No doubt she has a perfectly good reason. Like "I'm
not good with confrontation," or "You're better at the
emotional stuff," or "I haven't caused you enough pain so I
thought I'd make you suffer even more by ditching the most
important conversation we will ever have in our family."

[*Beat.*]

Rocco, sit.

[*Beat.*]

Thank you. Before I let you go, I want to tell you that I love
both of you and always will, no matter what your other
mommy does or who she schtupps. I don't want you two
feeling guilty or acting out.

[*Beat.*]

Rocco! What did I say? Sit. And no biting your brother.

[*Beat.*]

Good boy.

[*Beat.*]

Now who wants a treat? Whoever does their business in Mom Deenie's Louboutins gets extra food at din-din tonight.

Dostoyevsky Secret

Kate Huffman

KIM, 15 to 18

KIM *pulls her best friend Abby aside in the high school gym after cheer practice for a serious moment.*

KIM   Hey Abby, can I talk to you for a second? No it's not about our routines; our cheers are in perfect shape for homecoming, though your legs were a little bent on your back hamstring. But no, it's not about that. It's, well . . .

All right, I have a confession to make. Or, not really a confession so much as . . . a secret. Yes, I have a secret and I'm going to tell you because I trust you, Abby, and I know you won't judge me or run around and tell everyone. . . . Ew, gross—no, it's not chlamydia! Jesus . . . It's. Okay, just SAY it, Kimberly—JESUS!

I'm sorry this is so hard for me. It's just that nobody knows this about me. Except my parents—they know already. Okay, here goes: I . . . like . . . Dostoevsky. There, I said it! Oh man, it feels so good just to have said it out loud!

. . . Dostoyevsky . . . Dostoye—Fyodor Dostoyevsky! He wrote *Crime and Punishment*, Abby, come on! We studied for the exam together!

Yes. Him. I like him. I mean, I, I, I LOVE him! And I know it makes no sense. I'm a freaking cheerleader, and I'm deep into nineteenth-century Russian literature? And it's not just him! I've been tearing through Gogol and Turgenev and Tolstoy—all of them! YES! . . . I *know* it's weird. I mean, I'm not a dark person! You KNOW me! And don't worry, I'm not about to dye my hair blue and get a tongue piercing and start sitting with the emo kids in the cafeteria. I LIKE wearing cute clothes and curling my hair and getting hyped up for sports . . . but I also relate to something in this literature—like on a deep, human level. I've read *Crime and Punishment* six times now!!! So it's getting pretty serious. That's why I couldn't hide it any more.

I mean, think about Raskolnikov . . . Raskolni—the main character, Abby! Yes, the one who murders the old lady. He thought he was better than certain other people in society and that because of his superiority, he had the right to kill one of the "unworthy" people if it served a better purpose—the purpose of HIS advancement. How is that any different from football?? One team is certain it's better than the other, and they go out on the field to prove it! Then they get all this glory at the expense of the other team's loss! Okay, it's not a perfect metaphor, but you'd think it'd be enough for me not to feel SO DARN SCARED to tell people about this. . . . I mean, this could ruin my whole social life!

Oh Abby, please say you'll support me! Please still be my friend! Oh my God—really?

[KIM *starts to tear up from joy and relief.*]

Thank you! Thank you so much! And you'll stand by my side as I come out to the rest of the squad? Oh, you're so wonderful. . . . You're right. They may be weirded out at first, but in time, they'll come to accept me. I just have to brace myself for that. But better to be my true self. Aw man, I feel great.

What's that? You're gay? Oh cool. You wanna grab pizza?

The Slumber Party

Kayla Cagan

KIM, 15

KIM *is talking to her BFF, Jenny, at a coffee shop.*

KIM Jenn, you know you are like my best friend in the entire
world and nothing you can do will ever change that. You are,
like, the one hundred percent real deal, so please don't take
this the wrong way. But like, we need to real talk about Friday
night.

I know you are like, so amazing at party planning and I love
that you are throwing me the Total Ultimate Sweet-16
Slumber Party, but I feel like . . . there's a couple of things
that might be off. Alexis told me that Sam told her that Leila
told her that Vanessa told her that you wanted to make it gay
themed just for me. And that is so nice.

[*Pause.*]

No! Please don't be mad at Vanessa and Leila and Sam and
Alexis that I know about the surprise! It's okay! I think it's so

awesome and you're so awesome, but like . . . it's just not me.
I don't want a WNBA soccer ball cake. [*Pause.*] Oh, that's
basketball? See, I don't even know what that is. And I don't
want all of our friends thinking they have to bring me gay-
related or supposedly gay-related gifts. I still want and like the
stuff I always have: music, manicures, and ice-cream
sundaes—and I don't think any of those things are considered
gay or not gay. They're just awesome.

I don't give a crud about sports just became I came out and
Michelle and I are kind of a thing. Michelle likes volleyball—I
don't! You know I only go to the games to support her, but I
don't even understand how they score. They just rotate
around a lot. I think that means something about serving.

[*Pause.*]

Anyway, of course I don't want to cancel my sweet-16 slumber
party! I want to be with all of my friends and I want to be
having a blast with you, my BFF of the universe until we are
both old and gray and straight and gay! Isn't that our thing?
So, let's just keep being us. Cool? Slumber parties are just
slumber parties? [KIM *holds up her coffee cup and toasts Jenny.*]
Cool.

And the next time you want to do something really gay for
me? Maybe invite Leigh Ann Sullivan . . . you know, just in
case things don't work out with Michelle. [KIM *winks.*]

Poem

Alessandra Rizzotti

OLIVIA, 13 to 18

OLIVIA *gets on stage to recite a poem for the middle school talent show. She's nervous.*

OLIVIA   My name is Olivia Eloise. Entering in the alternative section of the talent show, reading my original poetry, typed on a Mac computer in study break, within 10 minutes. So here goes.

"Confession"
I wasn't going to say it
But I'm doing it
Here right now
You are my everything
I love how you express yourself
In watercolor class
Or how you cradle flour babies in home ec
You're like the sun to my moon
The can in my cannot

The rainbow in my clear crystal
My best friend
My crush/crushed ice
The cool rain in my heat wave
I would pick all the flowers in the world for you
So what I'm about to say may seem surprising
Or totally obvious
Probably obvious
Since I told you in a note one time
That
I like you
Will you go to the school dance with me, Adina?

[OLIVIA *stops, closing her eyes, afraid of the outcome.*]

[*Whispering to herself.*] Please say yes please say yes please say yes.

[OLIVIA *opens her eyes slowly, squinting, trying to not look at the crowd, then starts to smile.*]

Oh man. Adina! That's the coolest *YES* I've ever seen! How did you guys get together and do that so fast? Cheerleaders. Ha-ha. Ha-ha. So cool. *Y* . . . Is that a "3"? Kidding. And an *S*! Charlie's arms and legs look so uncomfortable. You don't have to hold it anymore, guys. I got the message! I can't believe you did that! I'm pumped! Thanks guys! You won't regret this, Adina. I bought the coolest tux so that you can do your girly Forever 21 thing.

[OLIVIA *turns her head as if she's been interrupted.*]

Yes, Mrs. Franken, that was it. I don't care if I'm disqualified!
I was using the stage to ask Adina out and she said YESSSS!

Weeee! Best day ever! Adina, so, like, want to go get Slurpees
after this?

[OLIVIA *turns her head as if she's been interrupted.*]

Mrs. Franken, you're lame. Teen love is in the air!

Thanksbringing

Corrine Glazer

CHARLOTTE, early 30s

CHARLOTTE *is a colorful, caring, and charismatic trans woman who is engaged to a wonderful man from an upper-class family that is tolerant, but not quite welcoming. In this scene, she is talking to her soon to be mother-in-law and having trouble containing herself.*

CHARLOTTE   Rolls? You're putting me in charge of rolls for Thanksgiving? When I asked you what I could make, I didn't know there was one word that could fully declare that you think I'm not good enough for your son. It's like you threw that entire phrase of disapproval into a food processor and out came one word. *ROLLS.* "Oh, Charlotte, you can bring the *rolls.*" Bring them, like I'd be picking them up at Walmart on my way over. Like I came from some trailer park. As if I grew up cooking on a single hot plate and calling free ketchup packets from McDonald's fancy tomato sauce. [*Beat.*] Well, okay, those last three things are true, but I will not be bringing you rolls from Walmart. You know, back when I was twelve and my dad became ill, we had a microwave for TV dinners, but in no time at all it became storage for late hospital bills and other past due mail. That's when I started cooking. But that's okay. You ask me to bring the rolls. I went to the school library every lunch period and read up on cruciferous vegetables and other alternative cancer diets. I needed a way to buy healthy stuff, so I bagged groceries and helped little old ladies to their cars for below minimum wage. When produce met its expiration, my manager let me take home a box load and every box felt like entering the gates of Disney World. I did so many school reports and science projects on eating for cancer that I slacked on any homework assignment that didn't have to do with it. The same day the school counselor called me in to discuss my failures, my dad beat cancer. He fucking beat cancer. That's right, my nutritious recipes cooked that cancer right out of him. But don't worry, you ask me to bring rolls to put on your Thanksgiving china. [*Beat.*] I went to college. Community school, but I picked up my grades and got a scholarship to my future. I was afraid to leave my dad, that he might get sick again, but he cheered me on, "Charlie, don't live a life of regret. Pack your rainbow bags and soar." I'm now a prominent food chemist and you want me to bring the rolls. When I came home for that first Thanksgiving in his new home, my dad said, "I caught the glitters from you. Charlie, my son, you're an inspiration and the only reason I'm here." He didn't say, "Bring the rolls." He knows I'd bake them from scratch, the same way every part of my life has been baked from scratch. From the moment I was conceived, through my transition, and even falling in love with your son. My dad told me as long as I bring myself to the table, I can be Charles, Chuck, Charlie, or Charlotte. And when I was scared before my first operation, he grabbed my hand, held it against my heart and said, "If you can take the heat of the kitchen, you can transition." Cheesy, but it was my everything. I treasure the matchbox cars and GI Joe's we used to play with and I still look forward to spending every religious Sunday shouting at football next to my dad with some wings and beer. So I'll bring the rolls to your table, Mrs. Jenkins. But I'll also be bringing myself to the table, whether you like my flavor or not. Rolls. Will. Be. Brought. And they will be delicious. And they will be glittered! That's right, Mrs. Jenkins. I'm making a giant cornucopia out of fresh-baked pretzel bread dusted with golden, brick-red, and burnt-orange edible glitter. I'll fill my glittered cornucopia with bacon-gruyere gougeres and honey-drizzled marscapone and pistachio pinwheels! Oh, it's not a party until my friends fig and fennel *roll* in! *Roll* out the red carpet for currant pumpernickel! Part the Red Sea for rosemary parmesan lavosh! Open the Pearly Gates for Grandma Jenkins, who loves her chocolate, and invite Jesus to one more last supper; I'm making Pinot noir chocolate rolls with apricot glaze! HALLELUJAH!

Death's a Drag

Leah Mann

DAME BEATRIX BUXOM, 50s to 70s

DAME BEATRIX BUXOM *is the ghost of a drag queen from bygone days. She sits in the upper level of a run-down theater, watching a rehearsal for the night's show.*

DAME BEATRIX BUXOM   I'm in hell. This truly is hell. For years, it was merely purgatory to haunt my old stomping grounds—nay, my home—but now . . . hell.

For this theater was my everything. My true family, my one calling, my life! Ah me, to have fallen so low! Life is a tragedy; but death . . . death rubs your nose it.

Look at these boys prancing about like schoolgirls. Where are the *women*?! They giggle and shriek and call each other "fishy." Well the whole bunch of them doesn't have the talent of a stinking load of scrod on the docks! How's *that* for fishy?!

DOING THE SPLITS DOESN'T MAKE YOU A DANCER!

They don't have the soul, the heart, we used to have.

Look at this ninny with her off-the-rack gown . . . she's not a female impersonator . . . she's a gross caricature!

In my day we respected women. It wasn't mere parody but *homage*. These young queens think *vagina* is a bad word. They don't spend time with real women. I learned everything from my wife and her sapphic lover. How to move, sway, murmur sweet nothings and belt out a number with the power of a thousand ovaries.

IT'S CALLED *SUBTLY*, DARLING! TRY MEANING IT!!!

And look how they applaud and encourage the talentless cow! It's wonderful to be a supportive community, but let's not forget the value of constructive criticism.

I would walk through any heavenly door to escape the pain of this. I'd happily wade across the River Styx or burn to a crisp descending the nine levels of hell if it meant an end to the mediocrity currently stomping and "singing" on my beloved stage.

Alas, I know not what keeps me tethered to this place. Some unfinished business? Impossible—I have none! My murderer has long since passed on and that was a lover's quarrel, nothing out of the ordinary.

[*Beat.*]

If you haven't been brutally murdered for love, you haven't loved at all.

I miss my friends, my lovers, my wife, the men who adored me, the boys I helped blossom into women . . . Everyone I ever loved or hated died years ago. There's not even a soul worth haunting here!!! It only has these so-called queens, whom I would sooner name scullery maids.

[*Beat.*]

No more. I shan't waste my energy trying to help the helpless. These little boys won't listen to a word I say and I haven't the energy to care anymore. SATAN! I SUMMON THEE! Drag me to hell! It cannot be more torturous than this.

[*Beat.*]

Oooh, I feel all tingly. That's unusual. I rarely feel anything but disgust.

Graciousness . . . I think . . . yes . . . YES! Praise be to heaven, I am released!

[*Beat.*]

And I am confronted not with brimstone but a joyous light! My prayers have been answered, my punishment for my plethora of sins—carnal acts, adultery, greed, ambition, hypocrisy, grand theft auto—is over! My agony here was not hyperbole but literal hell.

What is this? A heavenly door . . . it is pure beauty! Look at the filigree, the gold leaf . . . and on the other side . . . ?

[DAME BEATRIX BUXOM *watches as the door swings open.*]

Kabuki!

[*She sighs with pleasure.*]

Ahhh . . . . truly there is a God and her name is Craft.

Sugar Coat It

Ilana Turner

COACH, mid-40s

A male figure skating coach talks to his new student, a girl of 10.

COACH   You do not want to be a figure skater. You may think you want to be a figure skater, but you don't. You think you'll be glittery and pretty and shiny like a rhinestoned flag celebrating all things spectacular, but you won't. Let me spell this out for you: if you commit to the lessons you are starting here today, you won't have a life outside of this building. You hear that? That is the mechanical hum of compressors creating ice where it shouldn't be . . . potentially deadly Freon pumping through polyethylene pipes to take the only plain, ordinary water left in the state of Nevada and turn it into a sheet of ice. The slightly higher frequency, slightly more grating noise you hear is those lights up there—don't look up, they'll blind you!—those lights up there produce this fabulous jaundiced-color light. This garish glow will bathe you morning till night while you fall on your ass, which will, incidentally, always look bigger in spandex than you or I want it to.

And these kids out there, these will—save one real one—not be your friends. They will be your rivals. You may go to the mall on your limited time off, or have dance parties in the locker room when one of you sneaks a beer in, but they will always be looking over their shoulders at you when they land, hoping you saw their clean double lutzes, hoping your camel flew too far, hoping you jumped right out of the rink like Midori Ito at the 1991 World Championships. You look blank. You don't even know who Midori Ito is, because you're ten years old. She was the first woman to land a triple axel. If you want to be a skater, you should have a poster of her on your I'm-assuming-it's-Pepto-colored bedroom wall. . . . You don't know what Pepto is? Well, stick with skating honey, and you will. If you're lucky you will find one real friend, and good for you, you might get to keep yours. I lost my true love, Rob—a wonderful high-cheekboned, gentle soul who made love to the ice with every stroke of his blade—and lost many of my less-than-true friends, too, to a then new, unfathomable disease that ravaged our tiny world. AIDS, child, AIDS. Skating can teach you a lot more than edges.

You won't have time for real friends or boyfriends or girlfriends, anyways. You'll train on ice, you'll train off ice, you may or may not go to school depending on how fast you get good. You'll spend all of your time focused on getting good enough to compete for two to four minutes a few times a year. And unless you medal and medal a lot—and probably even if you do—you'll ultimately be training your childhood away to have my job. My job was lovely for exactly one year. When I first turned pro, I skated a show with Kristi Yamaguchi. I trained daily with Brian Boitano and it was right when the *South Park* movie came out, and all the kids warmed up to *that song* every day. They stroked around singing, "What Would Brian Boitano Do?" and it was truly hilarious because there he was doing what he always does: THIS. First stroking, then edges, then small jumps, then big jumps, then some spins. Even the great Brian Boitano has spent most of his life surrounded by floor mats onto which hockey players have spit and sweat buckets of *eeew*. In fact, Hopeful Next-Miss-Thing, even if you win the damned OLYMPICS, so named for games originally played by men with sculpted flanks in the shadows of a mountain on which the gods of yore sat, you'll still need moppet-headed comedy writers from Colorado to immortalize you. Only if you are eventually rendered in two-dimensional construction paper and beamed into the living rooms of every family in this land of liberty will your legacy outlast your biggest fall. And you will fall—all leapers do. So, the question is: Will you leap? . . . Figures.

Bi the Way

Jenny Purple

JESSICA, 29

JESSICA, *in fishnet stockings and miniskirt but no makeup, is sitting at the bar of a cocktail lounge talking to the male bartender.*

JESSICA   Oh, hell no! I'm not going over there! The next shot better be on the house for even suggesting it! I don't even know what I'd say! Yeah, right, dude. Just tell her that I think she's cute when I don't even know her. When I don't even know if she likes chicks? Or what kind of chicks she likes? What if I'm not her type? What if I'm not butch enough for her? Or too butch? I'm like a lipstick-less lipstick. Is makeup-free girly actually a thing, or am I the only one?

[*Checks her phone.*]

Sorry, the gay boys are late. They are supposed to be here to be my wingmen, to talk me through this, to be my grown-up version of the junior high love note "Do you like me? Check yes or no." And tonight was the night they were supposed to make this happen for me. For the first time ever they were going to help me act on my feelings for the first girl I saw that I thought was hot tonight. Now, there she is, and where are they? What if she leaves before they get here? If I don't talk to her I'm going to spend the whole night thinking about her. No matter how many pretty girls walk in here, it's her. It's my first time here. You know . . . new place, new me whole thing. How can they do this to me? I mean, I don't think they stood me up. I'm sure they're coming, just late. These guys have been my gay husbands for the last four years that I've been single. No, not like that—it's the way they take care of me. My men between men. Actually, we joke that one's my gay husband, one's my gay boyfriend, and one's my gay lover. Of course my gay lover is the one that kissed me on New Year's Eve at midnight, since among a husband, a boyfriend, and a lover, the latter is the only one that truly ever gives you any action.

It's so not fair. Why is it so much easier to gay-dar a guy than a girl? Gay guys either have a look or a vibe, just a certain energy about them. And I'm not just talking about the bear or the flame. Well, it's usually easier. I do have to admit there is always a fine line between gay and European. And there is that fine line between gay and the ultra Christian boy, too. And sometimes it's hard to tell if he's gay or just Southern. Or maybe that's just a side effect of the Christian chameleon confusion. Huh, maybe it isn't easier for dudes. It might even be harder. First they have to figure out if the man is straight or gay, THEN they have to decipher if he's a top or bottom. Now how awkward is that conversation? No thank you!

This is crazy. How can I be a Bi Fag Hag scared to talk to girl? Is rejection that scary for me? I'm never afraid to talk to men. Maybe I'm just noncommittal. Maybe I fear she IS a dyke with a U-Haul waiting to move in with me tomorrow. I looked up *committal* in the dictionary once. In addition to it meaning to be put in an institution, like a mental institution, it also means to bury a corpse. If that doesn't tell you something about what commitment does to you, than nothing will.

Okay, why am I trying to talk myself out of this? I'm always trying to talk myself out of good things and I'll never know if this could be good if I never try. Why does coming out have to be so hard?

Come on, I can do this. Just get me a couple of drinks, and I'll walk up to her table. For me. The drinks are for me. Both of them. Because, let's face it, I don't know what she likes or if she even drinks, which would make me look like a total lush. Women are more driven by emotions than looks anyway. How the hell do they ever hook up at all? This feels so complicated. Remind me why I ever came out to begin with because I really can't remember. Oh yeah, it was something about being true to myself or something like that. Gosh, I'll regret it if I don't. But if I do and she says "no," or hurts my feelings or embarrasses me, will I regret that, too? This is just my inner crazy talk. I've just got to talk to her honestly, like I would a man, except without the whole "I want to sleep with you" part. I think that type of brutal honestly only works on the opposite gender. I'll try to seduce her like a man, but be out for a best girl friend, instead of one fun night. That's kind of the best of both worlds, right?

Okay, quick before I talk myself out of it again.

[JESSICA *downs two drinks, one right after the other, and starts to walk over to the girl's table.*]

I got this.

Miss USA Choreographer

Jamison Scala

BARRY, 40s

BARRY *is an enthusiastic dancer turned choreographer who took time off from choreographing high school musicals to get these women into shape.*

NOTE: The actor should create fun dance moves to go along with the dance move names and perform them as if he's rehearsing with the ladies.

BARRY　All right ladies, Miss USA is tomorrow and this opening number has to be on fleek. If the high school kids I choreograph for on the weekdays can pull their shit together despite puberty and Snapchat bullying, so can you. So face bright, boobs right, and crotch tight. And 5-6-7-8, and 1-2, turn around, press the juice, and guide the plane, bitch-step back, and okay STOP. Stop, everyone. Miss Nevada, it's press the juice, not squeeze the tits. Squeeze the tits is after Orphan

Annie. When I dance, I like to create little tips to help me
out. So just remember, Orphan Annie was adopted by Daddy
Warbucks, AND THEN she became sexy because she was
rich. So therefore, Orphan Annie AND THEN squeeze the
tits, not the other way around. See?! Isn't that helpful? Now,
Miss Florida, you're home to the happiest place on earth,
Dis-ney-World. Please smile. You like you're from New
Jersey. Okay, not a dig Miss New Jersey . . . but, you know?
Right? See? Okay, good. And finally, Miss Alaska. Miss Alaska,
Miss Alaska, Miss Alaska. If you flex your foot instead of
pointing it one more time, I am going to take that Mt.
Rushmore replica behind you and shove it so far up your ass
you can sue Jefferson for sexual assault. You got me? 'Cause I
got you. And I want us to get each other. Good, we've all been
gotten. Please everyone, don't go near the craft service table.
If you even glance at a bagel, you'll gain five pounds. [*Beat.*]
Back to 1, ladies! And 5-6-7-8!

Severance

Corrine Glazer

HARRY, mid-40s

HARRY *is a serious and low-key guy who works in finance and is married to Jeffrey, a commercial jingle writer. HARRY was planning an adoption, when Jeffrey's sister's slacker daughter, Elise, dropped out of college and Jeffrey, who sees himself in his niece, thought he'd temporarily help her by moving her into the spare bedroom in their small 2-bed, 1-bath Los Angeles home. In this scene, Elise storms out and HARRY is in her room, packing her belongings, when Jeffrey enters to stop him.*

HARRY   Don't you look at me like that. I am packing her bags. Your niece has to go. Hand me that round scarfy thing on the chair.

[*Jeffrey refuses.*]

I know that you want to protect her, but she is nothing but a nuisance here. Have you ever seen her pick up her dish from the table and bring it to the sink? No. Of course not! I don't even ask her to wash it because I know she'll do it wrong and not understand the simple workings of a dishwasher, even after I show her that you can't stack bowls on top of each other or block the propeller piece. No, all I ask is just that she pick it up and walk it over from the breakfast nook or the dining room table or the couch and swoosh the crumbs into the garbage and drop the plate and silverware in the sink. That's it! There's nothing easier than that! Hand me the hoodie that's on the floor. Jeffrey, pick it up. She is getting away with murder here!

[*Jeffrey hands* HARRY *the hoodie.*]

I did not marry you so we could play house with some whiny, twenty-three-year-old brat. I want a baby. I want to adopt two adorable little babies. Real babies who need to be looked after. *She* is old. *She* is spoiled. *She* has no job! Playing video games is NOT the same as designing them. Don't you defend her! Don't you defend her, or I'll pack your bags too!

[HARRY *tosses Jeffrey Elise's backpack.*]

Here, you can start loading her games in this. I know she gets on your nerves, Jeffrey. Every Friday night, she knows we dress up for poker. And yet, every Friday night she gets into the bathroom before you to shave her legs for another Tinder phantom of the night. I know it pisses you off. Some twenty-three-year-old twat stealing your bathroom-mirror time, even if she is the spawn of your devil sister. Why do you think they kicked her out to begin with? I'll tell you why. She doesn't contribute.

[HARRY *notices Jeffrey is just holding the bag.*]

Jeffrey! The games aren't going to pack themselves! The quicker you do it, the quicker you can beat her into the bathroom to get ready for poker night. Is that a pile of chewed-up and spit-out fingernails? The girl needs a DustBuster attached to her ankles to suck up her mess as she makes it.

[HARRY *starts itching around the top back of his pants.*]

My poor vacuums! I broke two machines in the past year! Her long hairs strangle the motor and burn them out. Every couple of weeks I have to flip the damn vacuum over to cut her hair from the rotating brush. While I'm on it, it's not normal to vacuum a couch twice a week when you don't have pets. The space between the couch cushions is so tiny, and yet somehow among her cookie and cracker crumbs, I'll find her tweezers and nail files under there. Remember that time you were stoned on the couch and so excited you found a Polly-O string cheese under the cushion? If it wasn't for me, you'd have taken a bite out of her tampon! Yeah, yeah, it was wrapped and not used, but still. Our furniture used to look so nice and clean, Jeffrey. Look here. Because of you, we had to get her the most expensive gaming headset so she has the best audio experience listening to a bunch of thirteen-year-old boys making "that's what she said" jokes on *Halo 3*, and she dumps leftover pizza crust on top of it. If she were nice and dutiful, like Cinderella, we might find some mice friends here in her bedroom, but they probably took one look at this mess pit and moved on. Have you seen her collection of dried, sticky, pulpy glasses on her windowsill? That one's got a dead fly in it. THIS is why we never have glasses in the cabinet to drink out of!

[HARRY *finally finds what was itching him and he slowly pulls a long piece of hair out of the back of his pants.*]

LONG BLONDE HAIRS ARE EVERYWHERE! In my fresh-from-the-laundry underwear. In my socks. Sometimes they strangle my balls. And I'm not even into S&M! Yet here I am walking around, going to meetings at work with some kind of testicular cuff cutting off my blood flow. I CAN'T TAKE IT ANYMORE! Her hair isn't just strangling my balls and strangling our vacuum motors; it's strangling our relationship. Do you know what I dream about? I don't dream about climbing Machu Picchu with you or kissing you under the Eiffel Tower anymore. No. I dream about buzzing her hair to military standards while she sleeps. I'm going to set up security cameras. No, no, I am. I want to see HOW she does it. No one that sheds like that can still have a full head of hair. Look at your bald spot. She has your genes. Where's her combover? Sorry. Sorry, honey. I didn't mean that. She has me all worked up. I just . . . I'm setting up security cameras.

When I'm done vacuuming, I think she sneaks into the closet and removes the filter and just shakes her hair back out all over the living room again. Shaking it here and shaking it there. Then again, she's probably too lazy for all that effort. I've never seen someone be so lazy. Staring at our TV. Staring at our computer. Staring at our microwave. Staring at her phone. And those brain-rotting video games. She is barely a functioning child. In fact, let's tell our lawyer that we changed our mind and we are interested in adopting a child with disabilities. We've had plenty of boot camp training over here. Let's give a good home to a child who really is in need. We need her out of this room. This is supposed to be our baby room. OUR baby room. Don't you say it's a guestroom. It is not a guestroom! Not when she has occupied it for over a year! She should be paying rent! Our baby room, Jeffrey. Our baby room.

For Manifred

Leah Mann

HIS MAJESTY THE KING, 30s to 70s

HIS MAJESTY THE KING *addresses his army and loyal subjects from the exterior of his castle balcony before sending them to certain doom.*

HIS MAJESTY THE KING Loyal citizens, valiant warriors, beloved subjects.

[*Beat.*]

Today we go to war. We fight for freedom, we fight for our land, and we fight for love. In the face of darkness we will be the light. In the black of night I, your shining beacon, will lead you into the dawn. Some of you will die and many of you will be brutally maimed.

[*Beat.*]

Some of you will know what it is to send your cold swords into the hot flesh of the enemy. You will watch as the life drains from their eyes and it will change your spirit forever. Others will know the feeling of steel sheathed in your belly, the gurgling of blood in your throat as you desperately try to shove your intestines back into your stomach. You will see your comrades fall and know your women and children at home are mourning. Wives, sisters, and daughters will be left to fend for themselves, to scrimp for food.

[*Beat.*]

Some of your wives will undoubtedly turn to prostitution to provide for their fatherless babes. Your children may wither away or find themselves sold into slavery. Your mothers' wailing will echo through our villages. Our crops will be watered with the tears of those left behind—as this field is fertilized with the rich loam of your blood.

[*Beat.*]

In the face of this danger and inevitable suffering, you stand strong behind me—well, in front of me—steady in your resolve.

[*Beat.*]

Our enemy has affronted us most terribly. Every moment we wait, my darling jester—bringer of laughter and joy to my heart—is being cruelly held against his will.

[*Beat.*]

Manifred is well known to you all as the smile that brightens
our kingdom, and my dearest companion.

[*Choking up.*]

It brings bile to my mouth to think of our enemies chortling
at his pratfalls, despair to the pit of my stomach to think of his
witticisms entertaining their unworthy masses, and fury to my
brow that the nefarious, putrid King Xander should gaze
upon Manifred's most jovial and perfect of faces.

[*Beat.*]

Those of you who have spent time at court have been privy to
Manifred's good humor. You know well how he dotes on your
king with the passion of a loyal subject. You've witnessed his
impeccable dance moves. Indeed, even the lowliest among
you was swept up by the classic choreography he created for
my coronation, performing his work with glee around
bonfires, thousands of your arms reaching for the sky in
unison whilst you jumped and frolicked in celebration of me.

[*Beat.*]

I have my critics who claim this war is a folly, driven by vanity
and lust. Their spiteful tongues spew lies of Manifred's
fidelity. They say my love's freedom to remain in service to his
king is not worth thousands of lives—your lives. But I know
none of these critics stand before me today. You are the true
of heart.

[*Beat.*]

Today you fight for our shared future. A kingdom is not made up of one man, but of many—and it may not be righteously ruled by one, but by several.

[*Beat.*]

Self-knowledge is second only to love. I am your king, yes, descended from gods and destined to rule you, but I am not perfect. Nay, I am partially human and therefore flawed. My overwhelming sense of duty, of justice, and my dedication to my country have rendered me solemn and at times sorrowful. It is only with Manifred at my side that I can rule as a complete man, a man who experiences love and lightness in addition to the burdens of my position. Would you have a melancholy king?

[*Beat.*]

No! Would you have a king with an empty heart?

[*Beat.*]

No! Would you leave your kingdom without its very soul?

[*Beat.*]

NO!

[*Beat.*]

And so today you fight. You tell our enemy that we will not be stomped on! We will not be stolen from! We will have our joy back no matter the cost! Stand in front of me and face the swords and arrows of those who would darken our lands! Let your hearts be pierced by spears so that mine may be full once again! Today we dive into battle full of courage, our spirits lifted as we rise up and shout—For king! For Country! FOR MANIFRED!

Golf

Alessandra Rizzotti

STEPHANIE, 13

STEPHANIE *sits in band class. She seems to need to go to the bathroom, but she's clearly holding it in. She talks to a band mate.*

STEPHANIE   Is that an F-sharp? I can't tell these days. My eyes are getting a little messed up. The doctor says I'm growing or something so I need to eat carrots. No, I don't need to go to the bathroom. I just have restless leg syndrome. I'm not going to explain it to you again, Lily. There's no point if you don't know how it feels.

Gosh, when is Mr. Barry coming back? Is he smoking weed in the bathroom again or something? I'm itching to march already. I gotta get this energy out. My bassoon is waiting. Pretty cool that I'm the only one that plays this thing, by the way, isn't it? I wasn't going to say you made a bad choice with the French horn, but come onnnn.

[*There's an awkward pause.* STEPHANIE *has clearly offended Lily.*]

Hey Lily, have you ever golfed? It's become my new favorite hobby. Basically, I'm probably going pro at Claremont when I get in. I mean, I don't know if I'm in yet, but I'm pretty sure of my abilities and I just have a feeling that God is like, you're getting in, girl. That is, if he doesn't find out about, you know, me.

[STEPHANIE *lowers her eyes and whispers at Lily.*]

Lily, come on, you've known I've had a crush on Sarah for like, ever. I just never tell anyone because I don't want it to be blasted in our school newsletter that I deserve love and respect on LGBT Pride Day because duh, everyone deserves love and respect every day. I'm not the LGBT mascot of this place. Although, wouldn't it be funny if in band we had a rainbow as a mascot and a leprechaun chasing it during halftime? Ha-ha. So good.

Oh there's Mr. Barry. Finally. Yup. Smells like weed. I swear, if we weren't in art school with all the Waldorf kids from middle school, I'd report him. But, whatevs, that's what we get for having hippie parents. I swear golf saves me from this bullshit. You should try it some time.

I'm Very Anxious, so Here Are My Needs for Your House Party

Mike Glazer

DANIEL, 20s

It is nighttime and DANIEL, *anxious and sweaty, stands outside a front doorway, holding an RSVP card.*

DANIEL   Thank you for inviting me to your house party. As your boss's son I'm very excited and nervous to attend, which is why I'm in your doorway three days early with my RSVP. My third worst nightmare is my RSVP getting lost in the mail, and I show up unexpected. That's my third worst nightmare, number two is heights, and number one is entering a restroom where the only open urinal is between two handsome peeing men. Imagine having to make chit-chat with someone you're attracted to while straining to push out pee. Nightmare. Nightmare! Better to pretend you just came in to check your teeth in the mirror, and come back when it's empty.

ANYWAY, now you've got my RSVP, and since I'm here I should go over my plan for your party so everything runs smoothly. I've been to parties in the past where it didn't go how I needed, and I had to yell at the bathroom mirror until God told me to stop. I'll start with my arrival.

I do not own a car, but as you can see by the nine gold medals around my neck I run marathons. I'll be running to your house. When I get here I'll need to take a shower, BUT for your convenience I won't need a change of clothes because I've FedEx'd an outfit to your house. Just make sure you're home at noon tomorrow to sign for it; otherwise, I'm naked and it's your fault. Moving on to first impressions. Which way does your couch face?

Your couch faces the front door. Perfect! First impressions are all about winning the psychological war. You must be memorable and well liked. The following plan covers both those bases. I'll sit on your couch holding a small sword, making direct eye contact with whoever arrives. Ideally it's a strapping man, but whoever it is after we lock eyes I'll stand, shake their hand, and make a sword joke. We'll both laugh, making us fast friends. Then, I'll ask them if they're Jewish. Even if they're not Jewish, I'll sprinkle in some Yiddish when unnecessary!

I'm almost done. One more thing, then I'll let you get back to dinner with your tan husband and beautiful young blond son.

I do not drink. It is for *schlemiels* who believe a good time is had through superficial manipulation. I do eat, however, and will bring a two-gallon Ziploc bag of homemade mild salsa. Before I leave at eleven fifteen p.m., I'll use your sink to wash out my Ziploc for reuse. My salsa, your soap and water, *meynt sheyn got's veg.*

That's everything. Again, thank you for inviting me. I'm very excited, and not as nervous anymore. See you in three days.

Ethereal Epiphany

Darina Parker

MICHELLE, 18 to 24

MICHELLE is in her bedroom, getting ready to go out at night. She recently had sex for the first time with Tina (18–24), her best friend since middle school. Nervous about seeing Tina tonight, MICHELLE speaks to her reflection while she assesses herself in a full-length wall mirror. She switches from pacing to sitting as she acknowledges her feelings.

MICHELLE   Suck it up! Shake it off! It's just a drink with a friend, and not just any friend—it's Tina. We've done it thousands of times, there's nothing to be worried about, we're going to laugh and I already ordered crazy-topping pizza like we always do. What's there to be all worked up about? So, you went down on her in the backseat of your car last night and it was the best, most amazing sexual experience you've ever had! Whatever! It's no big deal. One doesn't just touch a vagina and poof! You're a dyke! Don't work that way. Oh my Christian Lacroix! What if this is a date? I can't be sportin' granny panties!

[*Realizing.*]

I cannot believe I had sex in the back of my car?! I need to shave! What am I even saying? Get it together, Michelle. Oh my holy Christian Dior! What if this isn't a date? What if this is the complete opposite? What if she's coming over to express rue and lament because I taste bad, or worse—that my performance was unsatisfactory. Nah! I smell like roses and taste like strawberries. Whoo! Okay! All right! I'm good, everything is good. We're going laugh, throw popcorn at each other, and at some point I will express my intense and unrelenting desire for her and we'll make out and she'll run her fingertips up and down my back and the nape of my neck and . . .

[MICHELLE *sinks into her chair.*]

Oh my God, I'm in love with my best friend. Oh my God, I'm a lesbian. Oh my God I need to shave. I'm freaking out! Freaking out, or coming out?

I've never felt this way about anyone or anything! Not even free designer shoes! I would birth all of her babies, C-section though—not sure Kegels would restore all the below-the-hip grip post-preggo.

[MICHELLE *shoots out of her seat and paces.*]

What is wrong with me? Two days ago I would've met her at a Governor's Ball in the same outfit I wore during a basketball game; now I don't even know how to BE in my own home?

[*Halts pacing and surveys her reflection.*]

Oh, my heavenly Christian Louboutins! What am I going to do with my hair? She's going to be here any minute. What do I do? Do I tell her how I feel, or say nothing? Hey, so I'm a lesbian . . . You are too? Awesome! Let's rub our bodies together. I can't hold it in any longer! I'm just going to shout it at her face!

[MICHELLE *hears a knock at the door. She checks herself once more and opens the door.*]

Tina, you're the only girl I want touching my girl parts with your girl parts—

Oh. . . . Well that *was* a fast delivery! Guess you weren't kidding when you said that thirty minutes or less part. Yeah, I'll just take that, thank you.

[*She closes the door.*]

Fried Chicken

Benjamin Ridge

DYLAN, 18 to 25

DYLAN *is talking to his friend Matt. The two are in* DYLAN'*s bedroom, which is complete with a La-Z-Boy chair and an overflowing washing basket.*

DYLAN   It was two a.m. I had just eaten fried chicken in my pants. I had been eating my feelings. Then I got a text. It was a dude that I'd been chatting with from school. We had only ever kissed by this point, at Stacey Rainer's party. Do you remember? You took shrooms and tried to discuss moral politics with a houseplant! "Sleep over?" he asked. I was excited because I'd never been booty-called before, from a man *or* a woman. Yeah, yeah, I know Matt! Middle school was tough. "Why not?" I thought?

I could've had sex with Dalena that night. Yeah, the one with the teeth. She was giving me all the signs. Intense, dreamy eyes . . . kissing . . . asking me to go to bed with her. You know, the classics. I think there's a moral reason people don't sleep with friends. I trusted social convention on this one. So, I told her no. Crappy social convention. My balls were feeling pretty heavy, you know? [*Pause.*] So, a stranger from school it was. I told him I'd be twenty minutes. Then he sent me emoji thumbs! Gross, right! [*Pause.*] Oh well. Better than my hand.

He answered the door and hit me straight where it hurts—my hat. "I don't like your hat," he said. Why do random hookups think it's okay to bluntly criticize my appearance! I wouldn't go up to an ugly child and tell its mom that it has a nose the size of the Grand Canyon! Even if that child was my own nephew. Yes, Matt, even if that child was my own nephew and its mom paid me to be nice.

I uniformly took my clothes off and put them in a pile on the couch, ready to leave. He had eaten cabbage for dinner . . . I could smell it. "I don't mind your nose ring," he said. Oh, well woop-de-fucking-doo for me! The thing is, dude, it's just a bit of metal in my face. I like it, so that's all that matters, right? Plus, I can hang wet clothes on it to dry.

He insisted I finish in his mouth. It weirded me out, man. I just think it's demeaning, for both of us. It's like a dog peeing on items of value. If I'm honest I was more concerned as to if I tasted like fried chicken? The position that I was in didn't feel very sexy. I was worried about my butt. Poo comes out of there. You know that fried chicken grease doesn't sit well on my tummy. Nothing really sits well on my tummy. Well, I certainly didn't know I would be in *that* position. Poo isn't sexy. Is it? Anyway, I couldn't finish. I had to think of boobs. [*Pause.*] Then, I finished.

In the morning I realized my nose ring had been weeping. His face gave quite a strong clue. "I didn't sleep well. You kept tossing and turning," he said. I didn't remember. "Do you drink coffee?" he asked. "Yes." I replied. "I'll make us some," he said. "NO. I have to go." I wanted to go. I might have said something that I wasn't meant to or that I might regret. Like my real name. [*Pause.*] I wanted it to end. As I walked out the door he called, "You would have a good body if you went to the gym." How fuckin' rude! I know I could drink less and exercise more, but *Call of Duty* is more important.

The first thing I thought when I stepped into the morning air was, "Can I still give blood now that I've been with a man?" They had such good snacks at the blood drive. Macaroons and Orange Tang. They have better snacks than I do at home. I deleted his number. I won't be visiting again. I wonder if his girlfriend knows that he likes the taste of cum?!? No, don't tell her. I'll post an anonymous note in her locker instead.

A Lifeline

Kyle T. Wilson

JESSICA, 30s

JESSICA *is on a difficult call with a crying caller in a crisis-prevention call center. She may be holding a receiver or wearing a headset.*

JESSICA   Serenity? Serenity, I just want you to know . . . I want you to know that I really hear how upset you are. And, and I'm sorry this happened but . . .

[JESSICA *is trying not to lose her patience.*]

Serenity, could you just . . . ? Serenity, could you please stop crying so I could . . . ? Serenity? Serenity, hold up . . . SERENITY, take a GODDAMN BREATH, Jesus!

[JESSICA *realizes her mistake.*]

Sorry. I'm really sorry. I know you're going through a hard time right now and I'm really concerned about you. I mean that. And I want us to talk about how to get through this. At least through tonight. Just . . . could you just stop . . . ?

[*Clearly, Serenity can't stop.* JESSICA *pulls the phone away from her face, a little panicked, struggling. Then she gathers her nerve and dives back in.*]

Okay, Serenity? Serenity—LISTEN TO ME. I'm glad you called us and I don't want you to do anything to hurt yourself tonight. Because you know who needs to be hurt? Who needs to be hurt is that loser dad of yours. You know what he is? He's a, he's a little bitch! He's a bitch-ass DICK! That's what he is! If that jackass is throwing shit at you and calling you a dyke, then that makes him a goddamn child-abusing menace! If I weren't stuck in this call center, I would hunt him down and skin him tip to taint! Gut him like a fucking fish! And that's AFTER I made him choke on his miserable useless flap of dickmeat!

And yeah, I know I can be a little extreme for a crisis-prevention call center, but I'm not literally advocating violence. I just have a vivid imagination! Never mind the fact that your puke-faced monster of a father doesn't have any problem with doing shit that causes you physical harm. I'm just, I'm absolutely FURIOUS on your behalf, Serenity!

Maybe I'm angry in general—maybe I shouldn't even be volunteering for a crisis prevention call center! But I'm not going to apologize for being outraged! How the hell else should I feel when shit like this happens? Why isn't everyone outraged all the goddamn time? Are you and I just supposed to shrug shit like this off? When your jerk of a dad fucking started it? FUCK HIM. If he's throwing things at you and hitting you, then he's a chickenshit coward creep and he should be in jail. The next time he does that to you, you pick up the phone and call 9-1-1. Or call us. Or tell a teacher. Or something. Hell—don't even wait until the next time. You're going to have to learn to take care of yourself in this life, so it might as well be now. Do it now! Talk to your mom about it, and if she won't listen keep talking to us. Or call the cops yourself! You have a right to do that! And I know that sounds scary and if its too much for you, I completely understand, and by all means, LET ME HELP YOU BULLDOZE THIS CRETIN! I will happily take down some info and get the authorities to put that menace in his place! You're a bi-curious badass, aren't you? Aren't you?! Well that makes two of us, Serenity!! Hell, yeah!

And guess what . . . You don't have to take shit from some mental defect just because he shot the wad that made you, got it? I know things suck for you tonight, but there are people out there who will support you and tell you how awesome you are. And some of them even have a Y chromosome! But most importantly, they'll help you incarcerate this piece of human waste, starting with me!

How does that make you feel? Better?! Yeah?! Good, cuz I FEEL GREAT!!

Chicks

Leah Mann

GABRIELLE, 20s to 30s

GABRIELLE *has a dry wit, a punk-rock style, and the butchest walk this side of the Sundance Kid. She sits down at a table full of dudes eating lunch.*

GABRIELLE   Hey, anyone sitting here? Cool. I'm Gabrielle. Thanks, man. How's the grub? Last job I was on, it was like prison food. Seriously, I've been in prison; swear to God, same cook. Shit, what did they budget like two bucks a head for catering?

[*Beat.*]

So you guys all grips and electrics? I'm transpo.

Yeah, I like it, pays good. Gets boring sitting in traffic sometimes, but the OT is worth it. Though when someone is screaming at me on the phone for oversleeping and the beef jerky commercial we're filming for the Internet starts twenty minutes late, I just want to be like—perspective bro. Right? I mean, in the scheme of things . . . let's all calm down. Low stakes man, low stakes. People need to chill. It's just beef jerky.

[*Beat.*]

Prison? Nothing man, possession. Stupid, I mean, weed is LEGAL now.

No, heroin. But still. Recreational is recreational, right? I'm clean now, though. Clean of everything. Seven years sober.

[*Beat.*]

I also beat up this chick. I mean, I was high when I did it. But yeah, it was bad.

[*Beat.*]

Oh, you've never hit a chick? Please, that bitch had it coming. She was sleeping with my wife . . . Ex-wife.

I don't need a code about hitting chicks . . . because I AM a chick.

[*Beat.*]

My name isn't Gabriel [*She pronounces it "Gay-bree-ul."*]—it's GabriELLE. *ELLE* . . . like a girl. With two *L*s and two *X* chromosomes.

[*Beat.*]

Fuck you—I don't have tits because they got chopped off.

[*Beat.*]

You never heard of a double mastectomy?

[*Beat.*]

Yes . . . like cancer. Cancer and prison. And drugs and a cheating ex-wife . . .

Awesome, right.

I got the dog, though, once I got out, so that's been worth it. My ex couldn't take care of anything. People who don't treat animals right don't deserve to walk this earth. It pisses me off. Seriously, like the way she treats animals and people, she should be dead. I hate her. I'd kill her if I didn't have family that would be hurt to see me in jail again. If it was just me, I'd do it.

[*Beat.*]

I know it wouldn't change the past. It'd still make me feel good.

[*Beat.*]

You eat cheese? You want this? I can't eat cheese . . . no man, take it.

Take the cheese. I know you're still hungry.

EAT THE CHEESE.

[*Beat.*]

Is it good? Man, I wish I could eat cheese. Good thing pussy doesn't have lactose, right?!

[*Beat.*]

I'm sorry, doesn't everyone at this table like vaginas? Well, me too, except I got my own.

. . . Why you all looking at each other like that? You think I don't see you? I'm right here. Men . . . whenever I think I can't deal with crazy-ass chicks, I remember you guys are dicks. Like I can't read your minds right now.

It was worse when I had tits. I'd be operating a lift gate or driving the truck, and without fail, some dude would be all like, "Oh, you can drive that?" I mean, what, do you drive your truck with your penis? No, you use your hands? Hey, look at that, I got hands too! Wow. Like my thumb can't press a button if I don't have balls or something. People trying to grab heavy shit out of my arms to "help" me when I didn't ask for it. Like boobs mean my muscles don't work. But even now, you're all looking at each other like, "Who's this crazy chick?" Soon as you found out I'm not "Gabriel," that's all I am.

[*Beat.*]

You know guys are crazy too, right? Some people are nuts . . . it's not a gender thing, it's a people thing?

[*Beat.*]

Oh, done eating already? Have fun circle jerking in the back of your grip truck. Let me know if you need help with the lift gate.

[*Beat.*]

Men suck.

[*Beat.*]

I mean some men.

[*Beat.*]

I mean people. Some people.

I Need a Dollar

Jamison Scala

TANYA RENÉE, 40s

TANYA RENÉE *is a Southern house woman with a thick accent who doesn't have to keep up with the Joneses because she is the Joneses and wants everyone to know. Her tone is a constant mix of passive aggression and sarcasm.*

NOTE: This character was written to be played by a man dressed as a woman. The asides to Virginia, Charlene, and Mary-Jo are digs.

TANYA RENÉE   Thank you. THANK YOU. Lord, it's impossible to find good hired help.

Anyway, welcome, ladies, to Clayton and my home. I don't think we've had a Women's Club meeting here before. I hope you noticed all the planting the non-American men did out front. I'd hate for all their hard work go to unnoticed. [*She proudly whispers to the ladies.*] Non-American is politically correct!

Anyway, as treasurer of our church's Women's Club, it is my duty to present charities worthy of receiving the money we made at last month's father-daughter dollar dance. On that note, we raised—drumroll please—one thousand four hundred twenty-seven dollars and . . . twenty-five cents. Virginia, please tell your husband he does not need to bring coins next year. It's a dollar dance, not a coin dance. [*To herself.*] Idiot.

Okay, so I have come up with three excellent charities worthy of receiving our hard-earned donations.

First, as you all know, when Clayton and I got married—[*She points behind her.*] there's the oil panting—my grandfather, Robert FTP Hudson Esquire III, opened a nonprofit in my name as a wedding gift. Queening Every Eligible Female LLC, a charity giving crowns to all the destitute and disenfranchised females—BORN FEMALES—of the South. Charlene is giggling because, yes, Queening Every Eligible Female LLC stands for QUEEF LLC. That is something my dear granddaddy obviously did not realize at the time, because his soul was pure—but Charlene has found some free time to notice. I suspect she's found that time while her husband is out at O'Shean's "fixing the jukebox." Who knew there was such a thing as a jukebox emergency. Hmm, Charlene?

Second, we have last year's donations recipient, and my favorite, Guns for Guppies, a subsidiary of the NRA. Putting firearms in the tiny little chubby precious hands of America's future.

And finally, we have the tried and true Girl Scouts. But now that their brother company, the Boy Scouts, is letting them tiny heathen homos in . . . I just don't think that's the kind of message we want to send to our children. Right?

So please write 1, 2, or 3 on one of these white index cards and place your vote in this stunning empty milk container Mary-Jo decorated for last year's vote. Mary-Jo, who knew macaroni could last a whole year? What a blessing. I'll be announcing the winner at next week's meeting. All right, meeting is adjourned.

[*She says loudly, as if there's chatter.*] Oh! If you have any more donations, you can leave them in the vestibule in the gilded clamshell I got from the Jacques Cousteau collection on QVC. Oh, oh! And don't talk to the non-American men as you leave—they have a moat to dig!

Cold as Ice

Jessica Glassberg

JONATHAN, 20s

JONATHAN *wears flannel pajamas as he lies all the way to one side of a king-sized bed, shivering. Multiple blankets are piled up on the other side of the bed. Half-asleep,* JONATHAN *pulls for a blanket, is met with resistance, and gets only a tiny triangle to cover him. He yanks harder, more resistance. He sits up, frustrated. He takes a deep breath, calms, and gently taps the blanket pile, which covers his partner.*

JONATHAN [*Whispering.*] Sweetie . . . [*No response, he whispers louder.*] Sweetheart. Can you . . . Can I please just have a teeny bit of the blanket?

[*Again, there is no response.* JONATHAN *more aggressively pushes his partner, and his whisper is anything but quiet.*]

Robert . . . ROB-ERT!

[*Again, no response.* JONATHAN *lets out another sigh.*]

Robert. Is this still about . . . before . . . ? About . . . Chris?

[JONATHAN *gently rubs the pile.*]

Sweetheart. I thought we were past this. I said I was sorry. I only asked you about going to Chris's wedding because I didn't want to keep the invitation a secret from you. I wasn't saying I wanted to go. I mean . . . why would I want to go to my ex-boyfriend's wedding? [*Flirting.*] Even if I could show off my superhot new boyfriend? In Hawaii. All expenses paid. [*Laughing.*] Way to rub it in our faces, right? We get it. [*Mocking.*] You have more money than G-d [*He pronounces it "gee-dee."*], Chris. You have stock in Google, Chris. You can have a destination wedding and not make it a total inconvenience for everyone . . . Chris.

[JONATHAN *turns earnestly toward Robert.*]

He can buy and sell me, Robert. Did I tell you, that was how he broke up with me? He actually wrote that in an e-mail. His work e-mail. Not even his personal account. His assistant probably sent it. [*Then, realizing.*] And that's what happened here. I mean, I'm sure he still had me in his Contacts and his assistant just sent an invite to everyone.

[*Drifting off, to himself.*]

I wonder if he still has Lucas. Probably not. Lucas would never have accidentally invited me to the wedding. He was so precise. So thoughtful. So great. He always remembered to get me the latest iPhone for my birthday and the latest Beyoncé tickets for Christmas. Huh . . . I should have dated him.

[*Laughing, then back to reality, defensive.*]

Not now. Then. Instead of Chris. Not that I'd *really* want to date him. Or Chris. Chris is getting married. It's a little late anyway. Not that I'd ever date that self-obsessed jerk-off again. Sure, I miss those concerts.

[JONATHAN *does the "Single Ladies" hand movements to try to get Robert to laugh.*]

But, I love dating you, Robert. I love how you smile with just the right side of your mouth. I love how we can always find a reason to quote Clue once a day. Or one, plus one, plus two plus one times a day.

[JONATHAN *laughs, hoping for a response. Again nothing.*]

I love how you always want to snuggle. Well . . . usually. I just need you to talk to me.

[*Again, no response.* JONATHAN *gets more frustrated.*]

But this. This is what gets so infuriating. This passive-aggressive bullshit that you pull. We talk. And talk. And talk until we are five cups of chamomile in. Then, of course, I apologize . . . every G-d [*He pronounces it "gee-dee."*] damn time. I'm always the one apologizing. Did you ever notice that? And you eventually forgive me, and then hours later here we are and I'm getting the literal cold shoulder.

[JONATHAN *shivers, pulling at the blanket again. It's all tangled. He then yanks with every break in the sentence.*]

And we have to start. All. Over. Again.

[JONATHAN *takes a deep breath; he is standing on the bed, yelling.*] I can't take it anymore! I'm going to Hawaii by myself. [*The final yank.*] I'm done!

[JONATHAN *gets the whole blanket. He finally realizes that Robert isn't in the bed. He searches under the blankets in disbelief. He turns his attention offstage, then back to the Robert-less bed. He flops back onto the bed with a scream that he muffles with his pillow.*]

[*He sits up and calls, lovingly, offstage.*]

Sweetie . . . when you're done in the bathroom, can you please bring me an extra blanket?

[JONATHAN *flops back onto the bed.*]

Portrait of an Angel

Leah Mann

ANGEL, any age

ANGEL, *strikingly beautiful, completely androgynous, sits on a stool inside an artist's studio posing for a portrait.*

ANGEL   I hope you don't mind if I talk while you paint. I'll do my best to hold still, but there are limits. It's an odd thing, isn't it, to sit for a portrait? You don't see much of that these days. Of course you do, but you're probably the only one. At the least, people tend to work from photographs rather than sitting in person—but in order to imbue the painting with my truest essence, I thought it best to take the traditional approach. After all, how often does one have a portrait commissioned of themselves?

You can understand why the Foundation wants a portrait of me. I am not only its founder but its heart and soul. I am the foundation. Its walls are built by my philosophy, its floors worn with the footsteps of followers who have been inspired by my very existence.

Are you familiar with the Foundation? I began it in
September . . . yes, of this year . . . yes, I suppose you could
call it last month. I was tired of people's expectations. As an
artist you must experience that . . . the weight of being
creative. I don't know if you're aware of my past, but I was a
well-known party planner. Being a public figure is exhausting,
but worse is the loneliness.

I know, I know . . . You're thinking, "But Angel! You were
surrounded by people all the time, everyone loved you,
worshipped you, adored you. How could you feel lonely?"

There's a point where popularity becomes a burden. I was the
"it" person. I was barraged by men, women, and everything in
between wanting to hold me, love me, caress me, be part of
my life—but it was impossible to know their true intentions.
With my power, I could no longer trust a person's intentions.
I felt used and alone. I wasn't a person anymore, but a
symbol.

And so I retired from the public eye. I quit the party scene full
stop. Yes, my raw sexuality continued pulling people in my
wake, but I was no longer the doorman to our fine city's
festivities. After days—no weeks—well, a week and half of
solitude and meditation, I had an epiphany.

[*Beat.*]

Are you ready? It's truly revelatory.

[*Beat.*]

My epiphany was this. We should only do things that make us happy. If something makes us unhappy, we shouldn't do it. If a person makes us unhappy, we shouldn't spend time with them. Our life is our own, and no one else's.

[*Beat.*]

Do you understand? You are your own person. Don't live for others.

[*Beat.*]

I'm not sure you're fully grasping. It's a huge idea. I've changed countless lives already. I know it's radical, but let it sink in . . .

. . . is it sinking? . . . Genius, right? Not to toot my own horn, but the world has been missing a philosophy like this and I realize it was not my duty—because duty doesn't make us happy, but my PASSION, my CALLING to share my ideas.

Now I only go to a party if I want to, and I find myself wanting to! If I sleep with someone, it is because I desire them and I don't care what they want from me. As long as I am happy, I'm being true to myself. It's been an incredible transformation. For the past three weeks that the Foundation has existed, I've done whatever I wanted to and I'm a more joyous person. The light just pours out of me!

You see it, don't you? It's vital that my aura be properly painted. Without it, anyone entering the Foundation's doors won't truly see the heavenly being I am and be inspired to join my movement.

[*Beat.*]

Helping others has made me so happy.

Britney's #1 Fan

Jamison Scala

DYLAN, 20s

DYLAN *is waiting outside a backstage door at a large concert hall in Vegas. He is Britney Spears's biggest fan and he wants all to know.*

NOTE: The tone is not angry, but rather intense passion that turns into devastation by the end. He's wearing the necklace and has the tiny bubble gum umbrella in his pocket to reference while talking about them.

DYLAN   Did she leave yet? Silence, I get it. Just like the guards at Buckingham Palace. Which is fitting because Britney Spears is THE queen. I bet you didn't think anyone knew about *this* stage door exit, mister security man. Well *I* know because I'm Britney's #1 fan. I drove all the way from Iowa to Vegas to see her in concert tonight. But more importantly, to meet her. Right here, right now. My boyfriend should be here with me, but he decided it was more important to take a bus to New York City for the rerelease of Christina

Aguilera's *Bionic* album at the site of the former Virgin Records
store. *RE*-release. *CHRIS*-tina. Yeah, you heard me correctly.
He probably won't be my boyfriend for much longer.

[*Casually.*]

So did she leave yet? Listen, I'm sure everyone's always
claiming they're Britney's #1 fan, but does everyone have a
necklace with a piece of concrete foundation from her favorite
Koo Koo Roo in Los Angeles, which by the way is now an
EZ-Lube and yeah, I drove there first to get my oil changed
in honor of Britney. I know it was out of the way, but it was
on the way. to my dreams.

[*Slightly frustrated.*]

Are you sure she didn't leave? Just let me at least give her this.
It's an umbrella I made out of Bubblicious Bubble Gum, her
favorite bubble gum. You're probably thinking to yourself,
"Why would you bring up the toughest time in Britney's life
when she shaved her head and beat in a paparazzi's car
window with an umbrella?" Good question, for someone who
isn't BRITNEY'S #1 FAN. Because any REAL fan who
REALLY knows her and can read the deeper meaning of her
tweets knows she's taken back that time in her life and taken
back the umbrella. It's no longer a time of shame, but a time
of strength.

[*More frustrated.*]

Just tell me if she left. You still don't understand. One time I
was watching my neighbor's baby and the baby started
choking and I was listening to "Hit Me Baby One More
Time" on my Discman and I just listened to the words of
Britney and hit that baby one more time. And that baby spit
up that hotdog it was choking on and lived. I saved that
baby—No! BRITNEY saved that baby through me. Like
Jesus. She needs to know!

[*Most frustrated.*]

Did. She. Leave. Just open the door a little bit and let me
peek in and see if she left. She has to know that when she dies
she'll become a saint and when I die I'll become her saint
assistant and when Kevin Federline dies he'll be reincarnated
as a tampon and when Christina Aguilera dies she'll just be
dead. Sorry Christina.

[*New, calmer approach.*]

Has she ever touched you? Can I touch you where she's
touched you?

[*He realizes it's not going to happen.*]

Okay, I get it. I'll go.

[*Devastated, he looks around as he's walking away, but is stopped
when he sees a piece of chewed gum on the ground. He pulls the gum
off the ground, examines, looks around.*]

Hmm, Bubblicious Bubble Gum.

[*Places gum in mouth and begins chewing.*]

Britney!

A Formal Presentation

JP Karliak

COREY, 15 to 18

COREY *and his best friend, Brendan, play video games in* COREY's *basement. Brendan casually brings up the topic of the winter formal, but to* COREY, *there is nothing casual about a formal.*

COREY   No, Brendan, I don't know who I'm taking yet.

Buddy, I'm well aware the dance is a week away, but there are multiple factors to consider. Not just any girl or guy will do. Yes, I'm considering both genders equally—it diversifies my options.

Like? Brendan, it doesn't matter who I like. I'm not physically attracted to a single person in our class. Not one. And the reason is very simple: we grew up together. These are the same people from kindergarten who explosively crapped themselves during recess. Rubbed ranch dressing on their faces. Ate nickels. And that's mostly the girls. Sure, they've developed curves since then, but I can't remove the image of them as barely more than toddlers leaking profusely from the eyes and nose—it's burned into my brain. And the guys . . . well, you know, male puberty and locker-room behavior is just a horror movie. Like online ones from Russia. It's sick.

Of course I'm still going! Yeah, it'll be a night without romance, but there are other benefits to attending the winter formal. Picture our classmates ten or twenty years from now, pulling out the old yearbook, flipping through, feeling nostalgic. They'll get to the picture of me and my date, and they'll think very specific thoughts. Was my date good-looking, did I "level up," does it make them a little jealous? Or maybe I went with somebody considerably less attractive, and then they remember I was a decent guy for "taking one for the team." And let's also consider not just what my date is like now but also who they'll likely become. If in ten years, they're a serial killer or a presidential candidate, those will produce very different reactions to our portrait. Well, at least slightly different. Without any romantic entanglements, I think it'd be imprudent not to consider all variables.

Okay, let's start with the girl shortlist: Hannah Prendergast. Pretty, we've been friends since second grade and we get along well, so I'll look like I'm having fun, which is key to good pictures. But she has very few aspirations beyond staying local and having babies, so in the long run, I dunno if that'd make people think I was remarkable for taking her. Grace is gorgeous, but will make every photo about herself and probably won't stick around long enough to get one with me in it. Olivia starts out pretty but dances too hard and becomes a sweaty mess. Sam is top of the class and is probably going to be something awesome in politics, but she makes a weird duck-lips selfie face in every single picture.

The guy list is shorter, 'cause you have to find one that actually wouldn't mind going with another guy. There's Carter, who definitely wouldn't, but he's so huggy that everybody would assume we've been secretly a couple for years and would look at a picture thinking, "Aw, they were so cute, too bad they didn't stay together." I don't even know his last name. There's also Eric, who's very smart, but he'd dictate every detail of the night. I hate people that overplan. Plus his eyebrows are too nice.

Ugh—it's so hard, though! Ya know what'd make it stupidly easy? If you and I just went together. I mean, think about it: we've been best friends since daycare, so we wouldn't have to explain anything; they'd just think we were buddies having a good time. Which we would be! We could even get a stupid prom pic together, and years from now, when I'm getting my award from *Forbes* or you're getting yours from . . . I dunno, *Field & Stream* . . . they'll show that great picture of us and reference how we both went on to great things! Great successful friends! They could even use that one of us from

Grace's pool party last year where we kissed during Truth or Dare. I mean, it's just such a random funny picture of two guys who love each other. As friends. Great friends. Or more than friends. Like brothers!

Of course I'm serious! Why, do *you* have a date already?

Hannah. I see. Well, Brendan, to be honest, I think you lack vision.

Fairy Godmother

Leah Mann

BLAKE, 20s to 50s

BLAKE *poofs into existence. He looks around getting his bearings. He's on a balcony at a party standing next to Edgar, a muscled, well-groomed, fit, and handsome guy.*

BLAKE   Well, hello there. You must be Edgar. I'm Blake. So, here's the spiel . . . YES, I am your fairy godmother. No, you don't get specific wishes unless I decide you do—I am here as a guide and an advisor. I am here because you either: wished on a star, messed with magic, or have been predestined for some special fate that you cannot accomplish on your own.

[*Beat.*]

You're really handsome. Pretty people privilege is real; how much struggle can you have?

Wait! Don't tell me.

[BLAKE *surveys the party inside.*]

Oh my God. First piece of advice, do NOT go home with that guy. I know he's eye fucking you so hard and he is gorgeous, but he's in the middle of a herpes episode.

Trust me. Fairy godmother . . . I know these things.

Don't look at me like that. I'm not some twee twink you can brush off. I'm here for a reason. You NEED me, so suck it up and listen.

[*Beat.*]

Listen to what? I don't know. What do you need help with? Whatever it is, you should listen to what I say. What's your big, like, life dilemma? Honestly, these days I usually help confused twelve-year-old boys with their "new feelings," and middle-aged men come out of the closet and dump their wives.

[*Beat.*]

What'd you wish for? I mean, there's no ugly-duckling issues here, so obviously this is a wish-upon-a star situation.

If you're depressed I will tell you that Zoloft has literally saved my life, no joke. I mean, I'm immortal, so I can't actually kill myself, but let me tell you what being immortal can do to your psyche when you're depressed. It's like super self-defeating and frustrating.

[*Sighs.*]

No? Okay . . . okay . . . let me figure it out. It's good to keep my intuition sharp. Do you need to come out to anyone? You aren't a secret bastard prince, are you? Because I can help you regain your rightful crown. It's been centuries since I got to do that.

[*Beat.*]

Ugh, then go get me something to drink. All your . . . sexy stuff is distracting, I can't think.

I don't know, ambrosia, flower nectar . . . whatever looks good. THANK you.

[*To himself.*]

Blake, get it together! You are not allowed to diddle your charges. You know that, you learned that the hard way and Esmerelda will not give you a fourth chance. Now think about why you're here.

His aura is all dark purple and sparkly. That's unusual. Purple means secrets, and one that dark is truly torturing his soul. Fun. I'll help him right his wrong. We'll be a dynamic duo making him a better person while spending lots of intimate time together delving into the deepest crevices of his being.

[*Edgar comes back.*]

Wine? A little pedestrian, but thanks. So, you did something awful and need help making it right. All I need to know is what deep, dark secret is haunting you.

Is it murder, because we can fix that. I've been part of dozens of murders in the name of the greater good—guardsmen, soldiers, evil stepmothers, false kings, tyrants, witches, this one woman Harriet . . .

[*Beat.*]

Plagiarism? In college? "Yawn," Edgar, "yawn." If you're going to cheat, at least get famous publishing a novel that you didn't write or win a Nobel for research you stole from an underling.

Don't wish on any more stars, okay? At least until you actually do something interesting or have something fascinating and horrid done to you.

And you're so pretty—it's a shame you aren't more creative. I'm releasing you as a client. You're a Goody Two-shoes. So unless you want to pursue an unprofessional relationship, I am out of here.

[*Beat.*]

Fine. Enjoy the herpes loser.

[BLAKE *poofs out of existence.*]

Feeling Suicidal

Alessandra Rizzotti

CHRIS, late teens to early 20s

CHRIS *sits in a therapist's office.*

CHRIS   Derek broke up with me. He said he felt like I didn't love him enough, but I swear I do. It's just gay drama. I don't know what he's even talking about, because two days ago I saw him with Terrence—you know, my best friend, the one I talked about in our last session—and they were flirting back and forth, singing *Rent* songs together. So I think it's more like he just wants to fool around. Which is, whatever—I don't need that. I could eat a Big Mac and it would be the same sort of unhealthy bullshit.

I know we were only together for six months, but I felt so lonely the day it happened, so I acted out and I went to the Korean spa down the street. And you know, sometimes the men there, they get aggressive. Which is surprising since their dicks are so tiny. I was offered some kinda pill. I don't know what it was. Probably Molly, or maybe some acupuncture herbal stuff. But I took it, and after about thirty minutes, I felt so dizzy, but free at the same time, like *Rosemary's Baby*. It was like everything felt outside my body. Every sensation was fuzzy and warm and it was like not stressful, at all, anymore. I called myself a Carebear to some guy in the corner. And he was this like small Asian dude that didn't speak English, so I bet he was like, "what are you saying?"

I was just feeling like I could conquer the world, so I forgot about Derek and I hooked up with another random Asian guy who had I think an even smaller dick. It was without condoms. It was scary, because I didn't even know his name, but at the same time, I didn't care. I really, really didn't care. It was as if I could just die that moment because why not live it up, right?

I walked home, feeling even lonelier. Like, bad lonely. Like the time my mom left me alone for a week at home without any money for groceries and all I ate was corn chips. And so, I felt like I couldn't survive. So if I couldn't survive, why not give up, right? Right then and there? I just had these persistent thoughts of wanting to die. Wanting to just end things. I looked through the medicine cabinet, but all I could find was my mom's Midol and her birth control, so I swear. O-M-G. I was about to take all the Midol and birth control, just to see what it would do. You know, because maybe all the lady hormones would kill me, you know? But, after I took them, I just felt sick, so I threw up all over myself, then peed myself and I swear, I didn't even want to change my clothes. So I slept in my nastiness. I slept in my mess. Being in throw up and pee was like dying, but not.

I imagine if I were to actually kill myself, I'd be way more elegant about it. I'd probably wear a silk robe, put on some Gloria Estefan, and drink myself to sleep with some sort of pills. I'd have to do research on it. Do you think I need to go to the hospital? I mean, I worry that what if, one day, I'm playing Gloria Estefan, and I just have the urge? What would I do? How do I remind myself that I am worth living and breathing?

[*Beat.*]

Are you shitting me? Meditation doesn't work, doc. I'm too creative for that shit. I'll just dance it off, I guess. It seems like the only coping mechanism I have is to be an artist. But seriously, is there medicine I can take for this? I don't know if I can be alone right now. I have to go to ANOTHER doctor to get medicine? What a waste of time. I swear to God, this whole psych industry is just a bunch of bullshit. You just want all my money . . . I know I don't pay for my sessions, but if I was rich, I would. And I'm going to be, doc. I'm going to be a pop star, just you wait.

You Need Therapy from Therapy

Jamison Scala

THERAPIST, any age

A THERAPIST *is talking to aclient in the therapist's office, which is located in a small metropolitan town in Anywhere, USA.*

NOTE: The struggle of the therapist is to honor the strides the patient has made in session while still not allowing the patient to think his absurdly homophobic ideas are okay.

THERAPIST   And it looks like we're out of time. Gosh that hour flew. Mark, great therapy session today, but I feel morally obligated to clear up a few things before I let you go back into modern civilization. First, cancer is caused by a mutation of DNA in cells. Cancer is not caused by two men having sex or "rumpy pumpy" as you put it. And two men having sex certainly wouldn't send cancer into the ether and give it to animals as you suggested. Gay men don't have the power to mutate DNA. That's not something they learn in their underground monthly agenda meetings, which by the way, also don't exist. Also, this may be a big shock to you, but President Obama is not gay. He's married to a woman. The First Lady. Michelle Obama. And to answer your question, no, I have not seen their wedding license, but I think it's safe to say it exists. Just like his birth certificate. Okay, you know what, that was a bad example for you. I take responsibility for that. And finally, we've worked so much on getting you to express yourself and I'm so proud that you were able to articulate this to me. But while I love that you used your words to come up with a creative solution to what you think is the world's problems, gathering up all the gays, making them wear rainbows on their sleeves, and then putting them on an island is a creative idea, but it's also . . . genocide. So, I gotta squash that one. So sorry. [*Beat.*] All right Mark, please see Stephin on your way out to collect your copay. And I promise you, he is not going to try to steal your soul . . . this week! Little joke. Okay, see you next Tuesday. And I mean that sincerely.

Own That Shit

Kyle T. Wilson

CHONA, 40s

CHONA, *a homeless trans woman, is being interviewed by a documentarian on a street in Hollywood.*

CHONA   You wouldn't believe what people throw away in Los Angeles. Computers, new shoes, nice new books! One of my best finds were these stunning McQueen suits, like pristine, still in the bags even. Two of them! One was this sleek reverse tuxedo, white jacket, black lapels. STUNNING. And the other was this scandalous scarlet—like blood straight from the vein. Found them in the dumpster and didn't even have to clean them. I wish you'd been there with your camera when I found those. That was a moment, I'm telling you! You should've seen me, I was like—

[CHONA *mimics a discovery—she holds up an imaginary garment bag, unzips it slowly, then—*]

AHHHHHH! The sky has opened, the clouds sing with the music of the angels, and Alexander McQueen has descended from the heavens! It's a miracle!

Of course they were like a size 3 so I couldn't wear them. So much for miracles. Even if I quit eating, these linebacker shoulders ruin me for couture. They were great when I was actually a linebacker. Those days are behind me now, praise the lord. But maybe it's for the best. Being homeless is hard on a wardrobe, you know. After twenty-four hours out on the dirty L.A. streets, that white suit might as well go back in the dumpster.

But God, you have no idea how badly I wanted to wear these outfits. I took them to one of those boutiques on Melrose to try and sell them. Went through like three places before someone got past what I looked like to what I had to offer. And I don't even think I look that bad, but I guess compared to all the fabulous people who usually go in there. If I looked like them, I bet I could've gotten more, but two hundred bucks isn't too bad for one find.

I've found more than that in cash, though—can you believe it? There was like this bag of cash at the bottom of a box filled with old porn magazines. The porn was in good shape, too, like a collection. It was vintage gay stuff, but like seventies vintage, leather, heavy stuff! I got nine hundred in cash and one hundred more for the porn, so that was a thousand-dollar haul! You'd think in L.A. porn would be the one thing people'd value. Of course maybe that's why the guy had the cash under the porn. Figured he'd never throw that out! Poor thing probably died and his sister or niece found it. Maybe his wife! Imagine it. They opened the box, recoiled in shock and just threw it in the dumpster to avoid dealing with it.

[*Mimics a discovery*—]

OH MY GOD, WALTER!!

[*Laughs.*]

But hey, maybe whoever owned it in the first place left it out on his coffee table for guests! I sure hope so. Screw his prude relatives. This is Los Angeles. Don't throw out your porn! You get to OWN that shit!

Parting Words

Leah Mann

ZEE, 20s to 30s

ZEE *visits his mother in her deathbed at the hospital.*

ZEE   Well, Mom, here we are. No, don't try to speak . . . save your strength.

[*Beat.*]

I said don't try to speak . . . don't—Mom, I don't want to hear it!

Thank you. Jeez, you got like ten minutes to live—don't spend it judging me.

So . . . I saw Stevie in the waiting room with the kids. You cut him out of the will or something? Man, that guy looks so miserable all the time. Think he's going to divorce Marjorie or stick it out? I think he'll stick it out. She must be great in bed.

[*Beat.*]

Well she must be! I mean, they've got four kids. That doesn't just happen. He's not with her for her wit or sense of humor.

[*Beat.*]

Yes, she does make a lot of money. That's true.

[*Beat.*]

Yes, she makes WAY more money than I ever will. So does Stevie. Their kids probably rake more in from shoveling snow than I do. . . . shhh . . . don't talk . . .

You seem short of breath, I'm just going to put this bi-pap mask back on . . . and there we go. Isn't that better?

Just nod yes . . . yes . . . good. So, what I was saying is that sure, I have chosen a path that is not about fiduciary reward, but about art and personal satisfaction. My life is broader than you could fathom. I have travelled the world. I've slept on trains with the Alps rolling by and performed on the streets of Tokyo. I've danced in the desert of Burning Man and gotten drunk at a wedding in Manila. I eat fire, I waltz with flames, I hula hoop with the gyrations of an angel. I—

Don't take off the mask, Mom—you need it to breathe . . . you NEED IT.

I am one of the most respected fire-dancing hula hoop soloists in North America. Is my lifestyle for everyone? Of course not, but it is for me.

Don't make that face. It's my life, not yours.

It's not that I don't love you. I do. I'm not sure why, you always tried to . . . make me "normal."

I mean, what's normal, Mom? A boring life? A part-time job with benefits? An apathetic husband? A kid like Stevie with his public notary business? Your cat that spends more time at the neighbor's house? I love you, in that weird you're-my-mom-and-I-can't-help-myself way, but I got to tell you—I don't like you. I don't think I've liked you since I was seven years old. I liked you before that because you fed me and read me stories. But at my seventh birthday you dropped my cake before anyone got to eat it, and when I got upset you cried instead of making me feel better.

It was always about you and never about me. That was the day I realized it. It was a pretty cake, too, with the dancing hippos from *Dumbo*—you know, in the tutus. You also threw away my tutu. That was not a motherly thing to do. Stevie got tons of sports equipment he never used and I couldn't have one tutu or tiara that I would have worn every single day.

Not that I'm bitter. I don't want you to think that. That would give you power over me. No, I am not bitter, I do not begrudge you your choices, I am forgiveness incarnate. I danced in fire and burned away your sins against me.

I'm not angry you cut my hair when I was sleeping so I looked more like a boy. It taught me that my appearance doesn't change who I am inside. I'm not angry you kicked me out of the house without a dime in my pocket. My years surviving on the street while you lived in the cushy home you never worked a day to help pay for made me the beautiful soul I am today.

I have nothing but gratitude in my heart for all the lessons you taught me. Yes, you made sure I learned the hard lesson. You destroyed me to free me from your grasp. You broke me down and I built myself up.

So yeah, I'm going to return the favor and help free you.

Enjoy your new journey.

[ZEE *pulls the plug.*]

The Extra Mile

Nina Ki

MAURA, late 20s

MAURA *is talking at home on her phone to Lauren Lee, a woman her friends have set her up with.*

MAURA   Hello, uh. Miss. Miss Lauren? Lauren Lee? Lauren? Uh. Can I call you Lauren?

[*Pause.*]

This is, uh, Maura. I got your number from Becca. The runner. Uh, maybe that's not how you know her. I mean, I'm sure you know who Becca is. She's your best friend. But that's not how I know her, I know her as "the runner." Ha. She. likes to run. Maybe I should have just said "Becca" and left it at that. Ha. That would have made more sense.

[*Checking watch.*]

Er. It's ten o'clock, right? Yeah! Well, by now you'll have received the three-dozen long-stemmed red roses that I sent to your office. I've heard a lot about you. From Becca, you know, and the others. I'm very, very excited that we'll be going on a date. To show you how excited I am, I've written you a song! Ahem.

[*Singing, off-key.*]

Lauren, Lauren, her name is Lauren. Excited for our date, it won't be borin'.

Not with Lauren, Lauren, Lauren. Just her name keeps me soarin'.

Lauren, Lauren, Lauren, Lauren. It's her I'll be adorin'.

When I meet Lauren, Lauren, Lauren.

[*Pause.*]

It's something I made up just a few minutes ago. Hope you enjoyed it. Uh. Here's my idea for what our ideal first date would look like. First, we'd have a picnic dinner on the beach. Something I cooked with my own two hands—nothing but the best, for you! And then after, we'd go for a romantic stroll under the moonlight—you know, feel the sand beneath our feet and the sea air on our face. All the while sharing intimate details of our lives. And then, maybe if you were up for it, we'd go back to my place.

[*Pause.*]

So you can meet my Gams! She tends to wait up for me when I go out, so she'd definitely be up. She's a real nice lady, and you know, I think you two would probably get along famously. She's taught me all I know about women, and the importance of romance. I'm real excited for you to meet her, and she'll be real excited to meet you, of course. So, uh—if all of this sounds amazing to you, like it does to me—give me a call! I'll be up until two a.m., I'm usually up late on weekends watching DVDs of the *X-Files*. Scully, am I right? Love those redheads. Are you a redhead, by the way? Or. maybe you're Asian? I can't tell, from your last name. Lee is pretty ambiguous. I guess I should have asked Becca. Though Asians could be redheads, too, I guess. If they dyed their hair, I mean. Either way. It's not like you have to be a redhead, or anything. Or Asian, I guess. Or anything. Except a woman, ha-ha, am I right? Lesbian joke. I'm. open.

[*Pause.*]

So, like I said. Give me a call! Or, if you can't today, I can do tomorrow, pretty much anytime, except from 12:30 p.m. to 1:30 p.m., when I have to take Gams to the airport. She's going to Vegas—she loves gambling. She won a thousand bucks once, on the penny slots. Wild story. I'll have to tell it to you later. But, call me pretty much any time before or after that—you can wake me up if you have to. Or, maybe I'll be up, waiting for your call. I don't know.

[*Long pause.*]

Shit. Shit, shit, shit. It was too much, wasn't it? God, I'm sorry. Gams is always telling me that it's better to wait, you know, to go the extra mile, and . . . she makes fun of me sometimes. She says, "Stop bringing the U-Haul to the second date, Maura," and I'm like, "How do you even know that lesbian joke, Gams?"

[*Sighing.*]

I'm sorry. I guess I just wanted this to be perfect, you know? Perfect for you. 'Cause I heard all these amazing things about you—that you're tough and smart, and funny. That you work in corporate management, and that you're ambitious but kind. That even though you're good at your job, you feel maybe like you're not giving back enough and that you're thinking of switching careers, to work at a center that works with special-needs kids 'cause your niece has Asperger's. I heard all of that and just thought, Wow, that sounds amazing. That sounds like my kind of woman. You know?

[*Pause.*]

I guess I should just quit while I'm ahead. Er. I hope that I didn't go too far with this, and that you'll actually call me back. I'll be waiting for your call. Heh. Or, uh, you know, not. Thanks for—listening, I guess. Your voice-mail box sure is long. Hope it's not full when you check it. Heh. Er. I do hope I hear from you. Okay? Okay. I guess I'll be *looking forward* to your—

[*Pause.*]

Gams? Is that you? Get off the phone! Yes, I'm calling her right now. No, I do not need help! No, Gams, please, don't say anything else! She knows I'm available, *do not tell her how long it's been since I've been on a* . . . yes, she knows what I look like. She does not need you to text her photos. How do you even know how to text photos, anyway?! Your pastor showed you how? I see. Great. Yes, I will tell her that story about the penny slots later, if she calls me back. But the chances of her doing that are getting lower as we speak, Gams—*please* get off the phone!

[*Pause.*]

Sorry about that. Now, where was I—Lauren? Hello? Hello? Why is it buzzing like that? What is that noise? Is this thing working? Hello?

[*Listening.*]

Okay, the limit has been reached, but I haven't said 'bye yet. I need to say—What do you mean, message erasing? No! Don't erase the message! Do not erase! No! No! No!

[*Punching buttons furiously.*]

Auuuuuuughhhhhhhh!

[*Listening.*]

Shit. Shit, shit, shit.

[*Hanging up, yelling.*]

Gaaaaaaaamsssss!!!!!

Love Makes You Do the Craziest Things

Cathy Lewis

MIDDLE-AGED WOMAN

A MIDDLE-AGED WOMAN *is speaking to her therapist shortly after the woman has come out to her mother.*

MIDDLE-AGED WOMAN   Love makes you do the craziest things, don't you think?

One of the craziest things I did as a teenager . . . Hmm, I think I was sixteen years old at the time. I pretended to be my male cousin Toriano because I was able to change my voice to a very low bass tone, like a guy. I got the name from Tito Jackson from the Jackson Five. I had a crush on a girl name Sherry, so I had my cousin Cathy, "ME," call her to introduce her to Toriano. Boy, did it work! lol Every day after school Toriano and Sherry talked on the phone and eventually fell in love. Man, I was the biggest "CAT FISH" ever! and didn't even know it lol. Sherry would ask Toriano every day, "When can I see you Torry?" She sounded so sweet . . . *ahhhhh*. So one day I came up with the idea, I am going to meet the love of my life. I had a big 'fro at that time like Foster Sylvers, remember him? He sung "Misdemeanor." Well anyway, I came up with the idea I would darken my eyebrows, shave the hair from my legs—I even got my siblings to donate their hair as well lol and I made a soft mustache and sideburns. I put a bulky jacket on and a sock in my pants and I was ready! I was doing drag and didn't even realize it LOL. I climbed out my window and headed down to the bottom of the hill where Sherry lived. Of course this was at nighttime, while my parents were asleep. I was so nervous, I was on my way to meet my future wife. Oh yeah, by that time we were talking about marriage and the whole she-bang LOL.

Sherry, her little sister Lisa, and her "MOTHER" were all waiting in the two-story-home window, when I arrived. I was nervous as hell, we begin to talk, and I spoke in my male voice from the sidewalk. "Dang, they really think I'm a guy," I kept thinking. They kept asking me to come into the house, but I declined of course. Our conversation flowed great for about ten minutes until out of the blue Lisa yelled, "That's Cathy!" I took off down the street with my sock in my pants frantic lol. I couldn't believe Lisa yelled out to me. Everything was going great and she messed it up. I headed back up the hill embarrassed and mad at the same time.

I climbed back in the window to my room and was a mess. All kinds of thoughts ran through my head.

Was my disguise blown? Did they know it was me, "Cathy"? Why did Lisa say that? Was my cover blown? etcetera. I tell you, till this day, it was never brought up who I really was. The very next day we talked on the phone after school, like nothing happened. I even told her I was on the same bus with her, describing what she wore—because I was on that bus as Cathy.

I thought about contacting Jerry Springer to share this story.

What do you think?

Should I? LOL

The things we do for love . . . . . .

Moving Boxes

Moll Green

CAILEY, mid-20s

CAILEY *is on a first date. She sits at a small restaurant table with chopsticks, two glasses of wine, and a little flower vase.*

NOTE: CAILEY met her date, totally randomly, at a bus stop. She really likes this person, but that randomness has her feeling a little nervous and out-of-control. Hopefully, the audience will be able to put themselves in CAILEY's date's shoes, and that's why we're not mentioning their gender.

CAILEY So, I moved here recently. New city, new job, new apartment. Moving is stressful. *I'm a very organized person.* This was actually the first time I've actually moved since I graduated from college. And—I don't know if I mentioned this already—I'm a very organized person. So, I had a whole strategy for keeping my stuff all organized. The first thing anyone will tell you about moving is to keep your stuff from the same room in the same boxes. So, the kitchen stuff stays with the kitchen stuff. That way, when you unpack, you can

do it room by room. You stay organized. And I had a whole
system. I was magnificent. I had these really *specialized* boxes,
and then I'd label them, exactly, with a sharpie, on the side of
each box. [CAILEY *mimes a series of boxes*.] Spices. Pots and
pans. Sheets and pillows. A box for novels, and another for
nonfiction. A whole other, more specialized one with a
subcategory: nonfiction, open parentheses, water pollution
and oceanography, close parentheses. And my system worked
great until I was almost done packing, but then I had to start
packing boxes that were just really random lists of things.
[CAILEY *mimes writing*.] "Old magazines, nail polish bottles,
cleaning supplies." "One frying pan, two T-shirts, extra
lightbulbs, a few pens, plus nineteen old CDs I was planning
to throw away, but in the end, I couldn't part with." The last
few boxes I started to write "Misc" for "Miscellaneous," but
let's face it, that's just not who I am. Moving is totally
stressful! But in the end it was just unspeakably *satisfying*,
unpacking all those boxes, knowing exactly what I'd find
inside each one. [*A beat*.] Which, I guess, brings me to you.
[*Beat*.] Because I'm all unpacked, and I still had a week until
my new job started. So I planned out a whole week exploring
the city: museums, the park, the art gallery. But instead, I
spent a week managing my online dating profiles. I'm
generally a pretty organized person, and I find I'm happiest if
I stay very strictly structured about online dating. I used to
just put the truth on there: single woman seeking men and
women. Men or women, that is. But now I know: the trick is,
you have one profile up saying you're straight and interested

in men, because you don't want to meet the kind of men who are looking for bisexual women. And then, you have an entirely separate second profile that says you're a bisexual woman only seeking women, because if lesbians find out that you're bisexual after the fact they'll maybe break your heart. [*A beat.*] Whole new city, whole new dating pool. Whole new data set to organize. [*A beat.*] Which is to say, I'm not . . . entirely . . . [*Wincing.*] . . . okay with how we met. I mean, "randomly" striking up a conversation at the bus stop? Not that you weren't very charming and everything, but it seems pretty random to me. I mean, doesn't it? I mean, and I hope this doesn't offend you or anything, but all I'm saying . . . It's just not usually the way I do things. *Usually.* [*A pause.*] I hope this place is okay. Is this place okay? Honestly, I was really hoping *you* would pick. But then, the way our text message conversation was going . . . I mean, it was a *really good* text message conversation. It had, like, *flow.* We had a rapport. I'm right, right? I mean, I'm not wrong? You were like, [*She mimes texting.*] "We should hang out sometime soon." And I was— mentally—going through my work schedule and unpacking to-do list for the next two weeks, but to buy time while I did that I was like, "K." And then you were like, "My treat. Wherever you want to go." And so I wrote, as one does, "Smiley face." And then *you* wrote, "That means you have to pick the restaurant." And while I was thinking of a polite way to say, "Oh, I'm not prepared, I can't, I'm new in town and I'm super busy and overwhelmed and under-organized and I couldn't even possibly begin to know how to cross-reference

Yelp and the appropriate local alt-weekly newspaper restaurant reviews in order to select an appropriate first-date venue . . ." While I was thinking all *that*, you wrote, simply, "I insist." [*Beat.*] Well. Like I said. You're kinda charming. [*Beat.*] So I thought . . . Japanese. Sushi? Most people like that. Italian . . . too heavy. Not just the carbs, but kind of . . . aesthetically, you know? So, sushi. I was slightly worried you'd have a seafood allergy or something. Or that you'd be a vegetarian. But then a lot of vegetarians these days still eat fish, so that seemed like a good calculated risk to take. I know I could have texted you back and asked you, but I . . . Well, I guess I kind of liked how simple and straightforward and confident you were, you know? And . . . I wanted to make you think I was easy-going, spontaneous. I guess I wish I was a little more like that. Like, if I wrote those text messages in just the right way, I might come off as more or less . . . *low maintenance*? [CAILEY *laughs at herself a little.*] Anyway, this is all to say . . . As first dates go . . . I'm—I'm getting my head around it. [*A pause.*] But I *am* glad I'm here.

Liberal Propaganda

Tiffany E. Babb

ALEXANDRIA, 18 to 22

ALEXANDRIA *is in her living room speaking on the phone to Kelly, a potential date.*

ALEXANDRIA   Oh my God, Kelly. I've been running around for the last half hour looking for someone who was not straight to obsess with this over. I just watched this new movie for film class last week. You won't believe it. It has TWO queer people in it! Two!!! And they're not even weirdly sexualized.

[*Beat.*]

Well, not *that* much, anyway. Definitely way less than your average Hollywood blockbuster.

[*Beat.*]

There was this one weird kinky sex scene that happened during a bank robbery, though.

[*Beat.*]

Why does Hollywood always think that queer people can't keep it in their pants? I mean, it happened during an *actual* bank robbery. Like, there were ski masks and lock picks and everything.

[*Beat.*]

It really sucks how few movies have queer people in them, isn't it? I mean other than the desexualized gay best friend or the *supertoxic* and sexualized bisexual and hot ex-girlfriend (which, I swear, I am sometimes). Like where are all of the normal queer people who get their own stories told? Where do they tell the story of a single queer girl just trying to get a date? That's where the real struggle is.

[*Beat.*]

I keep bringing this up in class, and the professor just keeps giving me this look like I'm testing his patience with my deranged liberalism.

[*Beat.*]

Serves his sexist, homophobic ass right.

[*Beat.*]

How hard can it be to write a relatable movie character who isn't a white man only interested in women, or a white woman

only interested in men? There's a whole world out there!
There are spectrums! When am I going to have a movie about
me? Just little old me trying to get a date for Friday night.
We're young and twentysomethings! Isn't the film industry
supposed to be catering to us?

[*Beat.*]

You know what? We should start a student org about this.
"Film Students Against Straight-Washing". We could picket
films that *don't* have queer people in them.

[*Beat.*]

What would our slogan be? "Stop straight-washing society"?
"All straight equals all lies"?

[*Pause.*]

"Your LGBTQA tolerance better damn well be
intersectional"? "Academics deserve something interesting to
write about"?

[*Beat.*]

Yeah, those last two weren't very catchy, was it? Obviously
someone else would choose the slogans. You're a good writer.
You could figure it out. We could make it a whole thing.

[*Beat.*]

We should talk about it over dinner sometime. You know, after you watch the movie. You should have been in class to hear people respond to it. I swear, every single person's comment had the words *gay agenda* in it. We should make a drinking game out of it.

[*Beat.*]

You know what? We should go watch it together. We can show those big Hollywood bosses that people *do* watch movies with lesbians in it. And maybe if we're lucky, we'll get to see the strange phenomenon of people watching the movie and doing their best to avoid enjoying it so they can concentrate on making mental notes for their future Internet arguments against liberal propaganda taking over the film industry. Ha!

Chubz

Josh Ginsburg

BRIAN, mid-20s

BRIAN, *a chubby young man, is talking to the mysterious man he
went home with.*

BRIAN   Your place is really nice. Like really nice. What is it
you do again? No, Brian, stop. Don't talk about work. Work is
not important right now. And you don't need to know my
name. Pretend I didn't say that. Names are not important. No
names. This is about. fucking. See, I can say it. "Fucking."
We're going to fuck hard. And it's going to be awesome. And
I'm going to love to be fucked by your. I'm sorry, I can't do
this. Am I talking a lot? I feel like I'm talking a lot. And I
don't know what to do with my hands. I feel like I'm
gesticulating like a madman. It's just, I don't usually do this
sort of thing. And you, you're just really. wow, that is a. well,
you have an uh. that's an eight-pack. That is definitely a. one,
two, three, yep, eight. I guess six wasn't good enough for you?
You have to look like a fucking statue. Is this like a prank?
Because you're like that. and I'm like this. and this is a whole

hell of a lot more than that. I mean, I'm like, I'm fat. Like, I'm fat. And, you know, I've heard of chasers. That's a thing. Chasers. But, like, you're not a chaser. You're a statue. No, no no no. Don't go for the belt. Don't. oh Jesus Christ. You're just a cruel prank made by God to make all of us feel bad about being alive. Is this the type of thing you call your mom about? That's weird. I shouldn't bring up my mom. You're naked. She doesn't need to be involved. We're just close so we talk a lot. I'm still talking about my mom, aren't I? I'm going to stop talking about my mom. So, we can just turn the lights off, right? Completely dark. And I can stay clothed. Is that okay? I'll just, rock this while you rock that? Because I'm okay with that if you are. Or, you can just stand like that. And I can just look. I'm just going to take a minute. I feel like I'm shooting like rapid fire. Just gonna breathe for a second. Okay. Okay. Let's do this. We can do this. I can do this. I can do this. I'm just gonna take off my shirt. So, this is me. And you're not running. You're not running. Okay, but for real, I feel like I should call my mom real quick. Because this is really exciting for me.

Work It Out

Leah Mann

GREGORY, 27

GREGORY, *a perfectly groomed man with a gorgeous gym-tailored body, squats and pliés in his workout clothes at the gym while a cop questions him.*

GREGORY   I told your big and tall buddy over there the whole story.

[*Beat, as* GREGORY *squats into a deep plié and then rises to his toes, perfectly balanced.*]

I was minding my business, doing my workout like I do every day. Not *every* day—I mean, Monday and Wednesday are leg days. Tuesdays and Fridays are arms and back. Thursdays are abs and chest. Saturday is extra cardio and yoga. Gotta stay flexible. Sunday is my cheat day. It's important to let your body recover. Do you go to the gym? You'd think cops would be in great shape—you have to chase bad guys, right? But no, you guys are always stocky and kinda doughy. I thought the donut thing was a cliché, but I guess not, huh?

[*Beat.*]

God, I would die for a donut but it's not worth it.

[*Plié, relevé, plié, relevé.*]

No offense.

[*Front lunge right foot, front lunge left foot.*]

Right—so the fight. Does spraying water really count as battery? That seems excessive to me. I mean, it's water and frankly he needed the shower. It's not like I sprayed him with a fire hose like you guys do to protesters. Does this look like Selma?

[*Beat.*]

That was before your time.

[*Beat.*]

Rodney King?

[*Beat.*]

Sorry, my statement. I'm doing my leg workout because it's Wednesday. And sure, maybe I'm a bit of a show-off, but if you want to build muscle and flexibility, the best way to do it is holding weights over your head while you do front lunges, followed by relevéing onto your front foot and raising your back leg as high behind you as possible. Like so—

[GREGORY *demonstrates with grace.*]

And yes, I do that the entire length of the gym because I'm thorough and dedicated. I'm not rubbing my body in anyone's face. Of course I have grace and presence; I have years of dance under my belt. If eyes are drawn to my charisma, I can't be responsible.

[*Right foot front lunge, left foot front lunge.*]

I'm minding my business, when that bro-ey douche bag tells me to—and I quote—"take my dance moves to the ballet studio."

[*Beat.*]

I'm not a violent person. I believe in beauty, art, love and brotherhood. But some homophobic redneck thinks he can bully me out of MY GYM—my home away from home—I'm not gonna let him go Stonewall on me. I'm gonna make like the Supreme Court did to Prop 8 and overturn his hating face.

I told him that and he called me a fairy and I called him a douche bag and he told me to blow him and I said, No thank you, I already have a boyfriend.

He said he's from Connecticut and a lawyer, not a redneck—and then he started to jump off his treadmill. So yeah, I threw my towel at him before he could come at me and he slipped on his treadmill and broke his nose. Not my fault he doesn't have my impeccable balance.

Then he gets up and comes at me, bleeding everywhere because HE smashed his nose on the treadmill. So yeah, out of the kindness of my heart I squirted my water bottle all over his face to help clean his wound.

[*Beat.*]

No, it wasn't JUST water.

It was water with lemon and cayenne pepper. I'm on a cleanse, okay. I *forgot*! My heart was in the right place. The towel was totally self-defense—

[*Beat.*]

I absolutely feared for my life, my physical superiority non-withstanding. Just 'cause I'm built like a devastatingly handsome deadly weapon doesn't mean I don't get scared. This is ridiculous. I'm pressing charges against him too—for hate speech, for threatening me, for being a pussy about a little cayenne pepper in the eyes.

[*Beat.*]

I know he's also gay, and know what? I don't give a shit. He's a self-hating gay man and that makes him a homophobe.

[*Beat.*]

MAYBE he's not self-hating, he's just ME hating. That's still a hate crime. If love is love, then hate is hate.

Did I not mention our history? Excuse me for not being one to kiss and tell. Or fuck and move in together and then have a hostile breakup where we said things that can never be unsaid and tell.

[*Beat.*]

I completely agree—violence isn't the answer, except when the question is a hateful little prick.

Jail? Now? Can you just give me another fifty-five minutes to finish my workout?

The Art of Cruising

Kyle T. Wilson

EPHRAIM, late 20s to early 30s

EPHRAIM *flirts with a guy at a party . . . by telling him how he flirts with guys. It's a little awkward, and* EPHRAIM, *nervous, is both cool and trying too hard to be cool at the same time.*

EPHRAIM   Most people don't know how to behave at parties. Bars. Whatever. I mean, wherever they're going to try and get laid, anyway. Not that I'm trying to get laid. Well, maybe one of these days. And hell, it's not entirely out of the question. Just so you know.

God, does anyone even meet people in person anymore? All that Tinder Grindr bullshit. Where's the fun in that? What happened to the art of conversation? Cruising? Human connection? It's imperfect, but it works well enough for me. Like tonight, right?

[*Beat, as* EPHRAIM *looks for a response, considers what to say next.*]

I got invited to this one party once, knew exactly one other person there and almost didn't even go. Second I walked in I locked eyes with a guy sitting awkwardly on the couch alone, clearly wishing he had someone to talk to. And there I was! That was too easy, really. Like a gift. Turned out to be a pretty cheap gift, at the end of the night, if you know what I mean. Learned a lesson with that guy. Never mind.

Sure didn't happen that fast tonight. I've been here a while. Was having an okay time but, I dunno, I was about to go home, honestly. Then I saw you standing alone. You should've seen yourself, peeling at the label on your beer bottle while everyone nearby had their backs to you. God, I hate these kinds of parties. Everyone planting themselves on the couch or clumping together and ignoring you. Of course they were kind of ignoring me too, weren't they? The good news is us social cast-offs got to find each other, right?

[*Self-conscious chuckle.*]

Am I being a chatterbox? And if so, is it working? It works for some guys, right? Does it work for you? I bet you use your friends or girlfriends, let them be wingmen or whatever. That's cool. Just don't tell me you use the whole male-bonding/camaraderie angle. That's so fake. Like all my internalized homophobia alarms go off when some guy with a baseball cap and a manicure starts calling me "bro."

[*Beat.*]

You don't really seem the type to do that, though. I would've weeded you out before now if you were. Yeah, I'd been looking around. Scanning the room. Surprised it took me so long to find you. Where were you all night, anyway? Must've been too many attention hogs blocking my channel. That happens some times. Like sometimes when I scan the room, some guys will look right back. Like they know exactly what you want. They expect it. They can supply it. They've got you figured out and they're weighing their options. I don't waste my time with them. They'll have somebody to go home with at the end of the night and it won't be me.

Of course I'm not always lucky enough to find a loner in a room. Sometimes I have to sift through the guys in packs. I like the packs because there's always one that should be singled out. Either because he doesn't quite fit, or because he's a little older than the rest. Anyway he stands out, but it's good if he doesn't know it. And maybe, maybe he feels like all the pretty boys' nerdy older brother and he's basically trying to keep up. You ever feel that way? Friday night at some hip bar and all the cool kids are running from one drama to the next and you just want to enjoy a drink with somebody who can talk about indie movies and like eighties college rock or whatever? God, I've been there. We're just trying to find a kindred spirit, right?

[*Beat.*]

So that's the kind of guy I'm looking for. He's just trying to keep up with some really vapid-looking pretty boys. Or he's standing alone, better looking than he thinks. He's anxious, oblivious of the possibility that someone might actually be singling him out. So when I find him, I just look. And usually, what I hope to get? After I show a little smile. Sip my drink. Wait for him to see me. What I hope to get is . . . it's not a look of confidence, or connection, or anything else like that. It's my favorite look. It tells me everything I need to know. It's exactly what I'm looking for. It's a look like, "Holy SHIT. Somebody's looking at me?"

[*Beat.*]

Yeah. You looked at me like that tonight. You looked great doing it, too.

Dining with Eleanor Roosevelt

Leah Mann

MARCO, early 40s

MARCO, *a drag queen without her face on, lounges on a couch, wearing pj's, talking to herself.*

MARCO   I should go. Yeah, I said I'd do it and maybe it'll be fun . . .

[*Beat.*]

Or at least not horrible. I'm not going to meet anyone in my living room, right? Ha-ha . . . ha . . .

It's time. It's time to get out there. Everyone says so and everyone knows best, right? No pain, no gain. Which is not true, because when Logan dumped me I was in a lot of pain and I gained nineteen pounds. Disgusting. I'm disgusting. I'm lazy and gross and this person isn't going to want me anyways. Who would want me?

Plus I'd have to get dressed. And in, like decent clothes. Not just less naked, but actually DRESSED. And shower, shave my legs.

I'd have to leave the dog.

I can't leave the dog. She'll miss me. She has issues because she's a rescue. I'd be a bad person if I left her while I go drinking and gallivanting about for my own pleasure. What kind of a daddy would I be?

But lord, he's handsome. I could use some handsome in my life right now. I'm not bringing it, for sure! Ha . . . I shouldn't be so negative. I'm not handsome, I'm gorgeous. I just have to put on my face. I'll feel better if I do.

Okay. I'm gonna do it. I'm gonna haul my lazy ass off this couch, I'm going to scrub off this malaise and have the date of the century!

[*Beat.*]

No . . . let's keep expectations low. I'm going to have a date. One of many, probably disappointing, but I'll have given it the old college go. Hip hip hooray! Etcetera . . .

Only he's expecting Violet Impulses, the velveteen vamp of Victorville and I'm feeling more Eleanor Roosevelt. What if I went without my face on at all? What if I went on a date as Marco, plain old Marco? In jeans and sweater with my glasses on? Ha! Wouldn't that be a fun surprise? Here I am darling! Au natural . . . love it or leave it!

[*Beat.*]

It wouldn't be fair, though, would it? To catfish someone who is probably a perfectly nice person and excited to date Violet.

Violet's ready to date. Violet's always ready to date, but Marco not so much. I don't think. Not yet.

Dammit. None of me is ready to date. None of me wants to leave this house for anything other than some Indian food, which would be fucking delicious right now. Leo, that asshole. He ruined me.

[*Beat.*]

This guy won't be as funny as Leo. He won't be as handsome or intriguing or clever or kind as Leo. Well, maybe as kind. Leo is kind of a dick, but the kind that made me feel like vibrating strings in my head and an electrical fire in my heart. I want THAT feeling.

[*Beat.*]

And that feeling won't appear in a plate of malai kofta! Put on your goddamn face and your dress. Stomp out that door on your heels and turn on the power because there won't be sparks without it!

[*Beat.*]

Or I could call Leo. Just to see how he's doing.

No! I don't need sex—I need a connection. A real connection with a person who has thoughts and a sense of humor. So what if I'm feeling Eleanor Roosevelt? She was an astounding woman. I want the kind of man who would enjoy a long conversation with Eleanor. Screw Violet Impulses. I'm going on this date, in my most comfortable clothes to have a meeting of the minds.

[*Beat.*]

It's going to be great.

I mean, not as great as my couch. Or that malai kofta. And the dog looks like she needs a belly rub.

Eleanor Roosevelt was incredibly ugly. Her husband had affairs.

Where'd I put the number for the Indian place?

QVC

Jamison Scala

CAVIN PITCHFORD, 30s

CAVIN *is an enthusiastic QVC host. Everything that comes out of his mouth is said with the sole intention of selling the product, but somehow his bullshit is sincere, probably because he believes it.*

CAVIN Well, enough about turquoise! Our next piece this hour is one I've been waiting to tell you about all night. It's item JO69FU, the Limited Edition Twenty-Fourth Anniversary of Washington Crossing the Delaware snow globe. Ladies and gentlemen, if you treat yourself to one gift this month, it has to be this snow globe. First, let me give you a tour. It sits 4½ stunning inches tall. The base and figurines are made of organic plaster and are hand adorned in the good ol' U. S. of A. And the globe is made of recycled glass from the Oklahoma City bombing of 1995. Now THAT is turning lemons into lemonade. And you get all this history for the introductory price of two hundred twelve dollars and seventeen [*Whispers* "seventy-six."] cents. Independence joke, ha-ha! Now home viewers, I know you're thinking to yourself,

"Cavin Pitchford, not another snow globe!" Well, turn the volume up on the television and let me tell you why this is so much more than a snow globe. [CAVIN's *tone changes significantly to a somber one.*] I'm sure you all remember three years ago when a former lover of mine began a LinkedIn smear campaign against me. Chills. It came out that yes, I am a gay American. That Godless man hacked into my LinkedIn account and added my first job—from what seems like a lifetime ago—go-go boy at famed Philadelphia gay bar Tops N' Bottoms. And to boot, he changed my profile picture to that now-famous meme of me performing suggested fellatio on ABC weatherman Sam Champion. Well, home viewers, I truly thought it was all over—everything I worked for, gone. But thanks to the wonderful support of all of you—yes, I read all your fan mail—and that inspiring online petition you started, I am still here today. [*Motions to ear.*] I hear my producer and best friend Shelly Buchanan tearing up in my ear. It's okay, Shelly—I'm okay! We're okay! Wonderful viewers, your love, support, and prayers got me through a terrible time. I faced the cold, I faced the fear, I could see the enemy in my eyes, and you know who else did that? This man [*Picks up snow globe.*] in this tiny globe, as he bravely crossed the frigid Delaware River to show the world he wasn't going to be stopped. And just like I conquered, so did George Washington, wooden teeth and all! I think we've all been G. Wash at one point in our lives. And I think we've all had this happen to us [*Shakes the globe.*]. This snow globe sits on my bedside table and every night before I say my prayers to

the good Lord above, I look over and I'm reminded the snow
is settled, but if it ever comes whirling up again, I can
conquer. And that, ladies and gentlemen, is why you need to
pick up the phone and order item JO69FU, the Limited
Edition Twenty-Fourth Anniversary of Washington Crossing
the Delaware snow globe. [*Beat*.] All right—up next is our
favorite crafter Renee Chevalier and her crafting sponges.
Keep it on QVC.

Two Sides of the Same Coin

Darina Parker

SCOTT, 17 to 19

SCOTT *lurks outside the bedroom window of Craig, his dearest friend through most of high school. Craig just found out through social media that* SCOTT *lied to him about which university* SCOTT *is going to. Now,* SCOTT *is doing his best to beg Craig to forgive him for withholding the information that in a few days he and Craig will not be attending the same university. On a warm summer night* SCOTT *stands outside of Craig's bedroom window and emotionally pleads with Craig's silhouette.*

SCOTT   Craig! Craig! Will you open the door please or at least answer your phone? Come on! Craig! Come open the door before your parents hear me and I have to run from the cops again! I still have grass stains on my Pradas from the last time. You're paying for new ones if it happens again. I can see your silhouette through your curtains! I know you can hear me! Fine! You want to do it this way?! It's not that big a deal.

So, I didn't tell you I got into UCLA . . . I'm sorry you didn't get in, but you did get into University of Michigan and I didn't. You don't see me being all sulky. I am sorry you found out from Facebook—that's not how I intended to break the news to you. I know we planned on doing the whole college thing together, but it's not like I won't be home during the holidays and other various breaks. Actually, you should come visit me for the holidays because it's going to be much warmer where I am. Craig! Come on! Don't act like a child—we're almost nineteen years old about to embark on the greatest journey of our lives . . . don't let this little thing come between us. How you weren't accepted to UCLA doesn't make sense to me. You're the brains, I'm the joke. You get the job, I get the laughs. We're two peas in a pod, two sides of the same coin. I don't want to go, but I have to. I guess I didn't tell you right away because once you knew then that would mean it was real and I would have to face that not only would I be separated from the greatest friend I've ever had (and not only because you covered for me that time when I blew up the oven in culinary class), but because you let me stay with you when my parents were going through the divorce, and made me feel comfortable in my own skin. Ever since tenth when we met that very first day and in a class neither of us were even supposed to be in, I knew I found someone special. Then the night when we came out to each other it all made sense why we had such a profound connection. And that connection has only gotten stronger and deeper throughout the years. It was like fate planned this spectacular future for us and we only had to sit back and enjoy the ride. Except, the ride is over and I don't know what to do. I didn't want to accept that I'm going to be thousands of miles away and only have your Facebook, Twitter, Instagram, Vine, YouTube, Google Plus, LinkedIn, Tinder, AboutMe, Tumblr, Wordpress, Snapchat, Flickr, Pinterest, and Skype profiles to fill the void that will undoubtedly form after the first few weeks. I guess what I'm trying to say is. I. I'm in love with you and everybody I love tends to leave, so I figured if I left first then you could never leave. I don't want to spend the last few days apart from each other. I want to do anything and everything or nothing as long as it's with you.

[SCOTT *hears a noise behind him. He whips around startled.*]

Craig!? What are you doing? Oh my God. I just remembered your text about your grandfather visiting and he was taking your room for the weekend.

[SCOTT *looks up.*]

Hi, Craig's grandpa! Great grandson you got here!

[*Back to Craig.*]

Maybe, we should take a walk. I thought it was strange that your silhouette was walking with a cane.

Fake It Till You Make It: A Classroom Monologue

Tyler Gillespie

DANIEL COLE, late 20s

DANIEL, *a high school teacher, is talking to one of his students, Billy, after class in his classroom.*

DANIEL Hey, Billy—I'm glad you asked to talk to me after class. Your term paper that compared Lady Macbeth to a TV episode of the wives-killing-husbands show *Snapped* was brilliant. And funny. You remind me a lot of myself at your age. I, too, dyed my hair blue and wore all black. I also never spoke in class. I was quieter than Justin Bieber sitting next to Neil deGrasse Tyson.

I get it. At your age, I hated my voice; it was super high and classmates said I sounded GAY. Now, I'm under legal obligation to not speculate on students' sexual preference, so I won't. Still, my classmates made fun of me so much for sounding gay that I wanted to disappear. I don't need to tell you this, but for all their good qualities, like brand loyalty and sneaker game, high schoolers can be pretty mean—present company excluded, of course. Y'all are a confused mess of raging hormones and social-media anxiety and take it out on each other. It's rough.

So rough, one might take drastic measures to change something he doesn't like about himself. When I was going through my whole voice-hating stage, I scoured Internet message boards for advice. According to one anonymous user, a famous rock star used to "scream into a pillow in an effort to make his voice raspier" and espouse that "throat infections will make your voice more grizzled." I tried this: screaming into a pillow and hanging around people with colds. But nothing worked. I still sounded gay. I eventually came to agree with one dream-killing poster who wrote: "If you want to lower your pitch, that would mean increasing the mass of your vocal cords somehow, and you can't really do that."

It's okay. Some people are just quieter than others, but I'm telling you about my voice struggle to save you throat pain and to pass on some advice: Fake it till you make it. My grandma gave me that tip a long time ago, and I didn't fully understand it until my midtwenties working at a science museum. I had to give five-to-seven-minute "fun" presentations in front of an IMAX movie theater audience of 314 judgmental people. One day my boss critiqued my performance and said that, even though I wore a microphone, I needed to speak up. When you've always hated your voice, this is the last thing you want to hear. What if the middle-school boys made fun of me as I was telling them about weather before the showing of *Tornado Alley*?

I ultimately got over my fear and projected my voice, because I needed to keep my job. Rent wasn't going to pay itself. Hearing my voice every day didn't actually make me like it any more. At best, I got used to it, and often, right before a presentation, I'd feel transported back to my what-if-the-middle-school-kids-know-I'm-gay anxiety. But I realized that, besides my Rihanna references, hardly anyone paid attention to my presentation. And more importantly, no one paid as close attention as I did. If people make fun of the way you talk or who you love, then they're the ones with the problem, not you. Don't let anyone ever take away your voice. I'm glad you wanted to stop by, and I hope I helped. I'd hate to see you waste your potential.

Oh, wait. What was that? You're in a hard-rock band and practice right after my class? That's why you're so quiet—to rest your vocal chords. That makes sense. Yeah, definitely. I totally listen to hard rock; I might even have a Pandora station for it. You just wanted an extension on the next paper? Sure, I can do that. No problem. And all that stuff about my voice insecurity—let's just keep that between us. Please don't tell your classmates.

The Siren's Lament

Leah Mann

CHARYBDIS THE SIREN

CHARYBDIS THE SIREN *is a drop-dead gorgeous siren who lounges on a rock jutting out into the ocean, sighing as she contemplates the emptiness of her soul reflected in the dark sea churning before her. A sailor is crawling up the beach to get to her. She eyes him wearily.*

CHARYBDIS THE SIREN   Alas, lo comes another sailor, crawling along my shore to profess his love. His broad shoulders and salty chest, no doubt heaving with his desire for me. His tanned face dark and tough like leather, his breath stinking of ale and poor diet. Big, rough hands pleading for my touch, followed sure as night follows day by the rising bulge in his pants. Majestic and proud.

How they love to flaunt their erections as proof of virility and devotion.

[*Beat.*]

What, oh gods, have I done to be thus cursed that I live in a world without women? Why do no women take to the seas? Must they remain the center of hearth and home? Bearing children? Stirring embers of cook fires?

[*Beat.*]

May not a woman wish to see the world? To explore, to conquer? I would lure a thousand men to their doom on this wasted isle if you would send me one single woman to warm my cold-blooded heart for a night.

[*Beat.*]

Or at least a decent conversationalist.

If I'm to be alone, visited only by frail dying sailors, send me one who's read a book or knows a few riddles. Forsooth, any being who'd speak words other than "Oooh, my fairest lady, my beloved, you most beauteous creature, let me bask in your glow and feast mine eyes upon your face."

Words which once uttered are invariably followed by the ugly man staring at me in oblivious adoration until he starves to death.

And those are the smart ones! Those are the ones who manage to keep their wits long enough to swim to shore and die at my feet instead of dashing themselves upon the rocks from a few notes of my song.

Not a single *brave* (and I use the term loosely) soul has washed upon my musky shore and queried me about my thoughts, or enhanced my knowledge with news of the world! I am not just a beautiful body and enchanting voice, but a mind!

Alack, this mind is but a pawn in Poseidon's army. He who viciously flings men at me to serve his own needs.

What of my needs? I remain intellectually barren and sexually bereft. Me, whose allure brings death! The cruel irony. I have wanton desires and they be not the coarse attentions of hairy-chested men. Nay, I dream of the soft caresses of a woman who, like me, has hills and valleys and the warm depths of the ocean inside her.

[*Sighs.*]

A comely siren such as myself should have the satisfaction of something more suited to my being than a MAN.

[*Beat.*]

Alas, 'tis not my fate. Maybe a dolphin will visit soon. They understand my nether bits more than some stinking sailor who's only had poxy whores at port.

[*Beat.*]

Or a porpoise.

[*Beat.*]

Yes, I could make do with a porpoise.

I Don't Have to Explain What Love Is

Alessandra Rizzotti

LIZZIE, 12

LIZZIE *explains the love of her two mothers to her friend Jackie, who seems to be distant from her lately. They are on the same soccer team, and they're kicking around a soccer ball on the practice field.*

LIZZIE Hey Jackie, I like your scrunchie. Good idea with the puffy paint. Anyways, enough small talk. Do you have a second to talk real stuff? Let's do some dribbling. You go over there and I'll pass you the ball. Don't be scared, I'm just going to get real with you, which you need to learn how to do eventually anyways.

[LIZZIE *kicks the ball toward Jackie and tries to corner her at the end of the field.*]

So, I heard you talking about my moms, and I'm just confused, because I thought you were my friend. Can I ask why you think it's weird for me to have two moms? Or do I need to scientifically explain that no, one of my moms is not my genetic mom, but she's raising me, so she's my mom, and no, I don't know the dad because he was just a sperm. Are you even in sex ed yet? You'll learn that when you get there.

[LIZZIE *starts to kick the ball upwards, like a hacky sack.*]

Jackie, I KNOW you're Christian. We go to the same church. That's probably why you think kissing is sex. But guess what, everyone has sex eventually, and if we didn't, we wouldn't exist. And good news is, Jesus loves everyone, including gays, so accept that he is into everyone. I know the bumper stickers say "Jesus Loves You," but when they say "you," they mean everyone, not just YOU. Jackie, you gotta improve your footwork. Your legs look like spaghetti. Just my two cents, but what do I know?

And to address your cafeteria Q & A about lesbian vs. straight couples, my moms don't kiss more than your mom and dad just because they're lesbians, Jackie. People who are in love express love in different ways. Some do it with gifts like dumb teddy bears, some do it by holding hands, some do it by doing laundry for each other, some do it by not screaming at each other. I don't know if your parents kiss at all (I'm assuming they don't, since you seem weird about it), but people who love each other do things like kissing (preferably in private). You act like they kiss in front of your face all the time like weird teenagers at a movie theater, and I've never seen them do that, so why are you making that up?

Being mean and talking behind people's backs is not cool, even if you're popular and have the best Demi Lovato binders. My moms deserve as much respect as your parents do, especially because my moms actually care about our school and do so much for us, whether it's at the PTA or in our classrooms, cutting construction paper, grading papers, and making soccer snacks. Which by the way, watch out. If you continue to be mean like you have been, they might just give you poisoned crackers.

[LIZZIE *kicks the ball toward Jackie.*]

Kidding. Have a good night. Think about your words before you say them. You're not a puppet. You have the power to change.

[LIZZIE *notices that Jackie seems down now.*]

Oh come on, turn that frown upside down! You have a cool scrunchie AND it matches our uniforms. I can't even match my socks. May peace be with you and let's beat those Tigers this weekend, eh?

[LIZZIE *kicks the ball toward Jackie.*]

Obsessed with Odor in the Air

Libby Doyne

JIMMY, 30s

JIMMY is in the cockpit of a commercial airplane, piloting a daytime flight. A static noise, and then JIMMY *speaking to his passengers, can be heard through the sound system of the plane.*

JIMMY   Good morning passengers, this is your pilot speaking. We have now reached a comfortable cruising altitude, so we've gone ahead and turned off the Fasten Seat Belt sign, though we do recommended you keep your seat belt tightly fastened and remain seated for the duration of the flight.

Okay, you guys—I want to let you know right off the bat that I have a very sensitive sense of smell. So if you've packed any food, please for the love of God just wait until you get off the plane. It's a two-hour flight—can you really not go two hours without eating?!

As of right now, we're on track to touch down in Phoenix at 2:48, that's about ten minutes ahead of schedule due to the jet stream. You know what? I just cannot continue, because I am getting a stream of vile foot stank straight into my damn nostril right now. What a putrid stench, I mean, who takes off their shoes in a small, enclosed tube with recycled air? Sweet Jesus, almighty.

Breathe, Jimmy. Breathe. . . . If you look out the window in a just a minute, you'll be able to see the Grand Canyon on the left side of the aircraft. Just a fair warning, we may experience a bit of turbulence up ahead due to a north-northeast wind, so don't be alarmed.

Speaking of wind, you guys, I know turbulence can unexpectedly jostle a fart right out of you, but please try your damnedest to hold it in real tight. Do that for me, will you, sweetie? I don't want to have to release the oxygen masks up in this bitch just to get a breath of fresh air.

In the event oxygen masks are released, do remember to place the mask firmly over your mouth and pull the strings to tightly fasten. The bags may not inflate.

I've got it. You know what it smells like in here right now? Sauerkraut. IT. SMELLS. LIKE. SAUERKRAUT. IN. HERE. Brings me right back to those days when I was piloting the Lufthansa fleet. That's where I met my husband, Dolf. He was a flight attendant, and I fell in love the moment

I saw him flush a stinky bag of that putrid cabbage soaked in vinegar right down the toilet. *WOOSH!* After the flight I told him he was the wind beneath my wings and a week later we were mackin' on the tarmack. Ohhh, that smell! I am beside myself. Just kidding—my copilot is beside me . . . HAH!

You know what, I'm going to turn this DAMN PLANE AROUND. Someone is actually eating Limburger cheese in my aircraft. I suggest you wrap that thing up, sir! Put it in the OVERHEAD COMPARTMENT.

Though do use caution when opening the overhead compartment, as your items may have shifted during takeoff.

Again, thank you for flying Delta Airlines—more like SMELLta Airlines, am I right? Okay, byeeeeee!

The Problem Is . . .
(The Starbucks Monologue)

Tiffany E. Babb

IRENE, 18 to 27

IRENE *is in the park. She is speaking to Jesse, a 10-year-old child who Irene is babysitting.*

IRENE   So there is this *very* cute girl who works at Starbucks. And I swear, I'm not actually stalking her.

[*Beat.*]

She definitely thinks I'm stalking her.

[*Beat.*]

The problem is, every time I see this girl, I get in these really strangely awkward situations. Like, the things that are happening would be fine or maybe even a little bit funny if it were with someone I knew or were even friendly with. But the fact that we're both strangers?

[*Beat.*]

It makes things weird.

[*Beat.*]

You want an example? Okay. So I was sitting inside Starbucks near-*ish* to the door one day. And out of my peripheral vision, I see someone outside struggling to open the door. When I get up to help, I realize that it's this girl, right? She's lugging two bags of ice into the store from her car.

[*Beat.*]

So I open the door for her, smile, she says "Thank you," I say "No problem," and all is well and good, right? Except not really. Because once I sit back down at my laptop and get my earbuds back in, I realize that she's heading back out for *another* trip to get ice. And of course I get up to help her with the door again. It would be strange if I helped her the first time and *didn't* the second time. But at this point, it's already getting weird.

[*Beat.*]

And then it happens again. . . . And again.

[*Beat.*]

By the time she's finished lugging eight or so bags into the store, we're both dying of awkwardness.

[*Beat.*]

Last week she dropped a stack of cups, and I rushed to help her pick them up and almost knocked her over.

[*Beat.*]

And that's not where it ends. No sir. Today I was picking up little Tommy, that other kid I babysit, from school, and I didn't want to deal with the parental gridlock in front of the school, so I told him to go find me around the corner in front of this big apartment building. So I was there, sitting outside of the apartments, waiting creepily, when SHE walks out of the building, gives me a weird look, and then takes off on her motorcycle. *Yes*, she rides a motorcycle. She is so *cool*.

[*Beat.*]

I was talking to one of the other baristas that I know, and, like, apparently, that's the actual building that she lives in. She probably thinks that I'm some sort of creepy stalker now that I know where she lives. Talking to her coworkers about where she lives also probably doesn't help.

[*Beat.*]

Anyway. It would be really weird for me to ask her out at this point, right? Yeah. It probably would be. And I don't even know if she likes women. She did wear one of those rainbow equality pins during Pride, but everyone has one of *those* these days.

[*Beat.*]

What if you came with me one day, and talked to her for me? You could help me find out whether or not she is into women! And you could convince her that I am a totally normal, totally dateable person.

[*Beat.*]

Yeah, maybe your mom wouldn't think that was a good idea. *Hmph.* Maybe she'll come with me.

Game Over

Leah Mann

DWAYNE THE ZOMBIE, 20s to 40s

DWAYNE THE ZOMBIE *sits huddled in the corner of an abandoned building with his boyfriend,* Andre *(who is not a zombie). Chaos reigns outside, but the two have each other.*

DWAYNE THE ZOMBIE   Fuck.

[*Beat.*]

I think it's going to be time soon.

[*Beat.*]

Don't say nothing, I mean it. Listen to me—I wouldn't have made it this long without you. You know you're my everything, but we've got, what, a day or two at most before I'm slobbering over your brains instead of your gorgeous body?

[*Beat.*]

You remember when we met? Semifinals junior year. You were point guard, and damn! Your moves! I was up in that booth calling the game and couldn't do nothing but watch you. I missed a three pointer and a foul 'cause I was staring at your ass down on the court.

[DWAYNE *stops speaking, listening to screams outside.*]

Someone just went down.

[*Beat.*]

I don't think I would have made it through high school if it weren't for you. Yeah, my grades were straight As, I was student council president, ran the radio station, DJ'd every dance, and my dad was the principal—but you kept my head on straight . . . ha, get it? Straight? That's funny 'cause I ain't been straight since the day I popped out my momma. I mean, if it weren't for you I'd have left Virginia, gone to Stanford, gotten my law degree, and taken that job working for my uncle at the Supreme Court.

[*Beat.*]

But instead I got you and I don't have a single damned regret. You gave me love, joy, lightness in my heart, and euphoria in my cock. You make my eyes twinkle and chest thump and my blood rush. You give me humanity and got me my start in the entertainment biz. My parents may think getting coffee, dry cleaning, and picking the poppy seeds off of bagels for the host of a shopping network segment producer is a waste of my talents, but you see the true me.

[*Beat.*]

I'm starting to feel tingly. Eww . . . look at my foot. That's nasty. It's just dangling there.

[DWAYNE *reaches down and touches his foot. It comes off in his hand.*]

Eww.

[*Beat.*]

What was I sayin'? Right, you see the true me. The me who has dreams and passion and the ability to do any job, no matter how small, if it means being close to the one I love while he pursues his dream of bringing competitive arm wrestling into every school.

[*Beat.*]

Baby, don't cry. I'm not saying all this to say good-bye. I'm saying it to say thank you. I won't have your brain go to waste. You always did what was in my best interest. Pushing me in front of you while the zombie horde was climbing down the chimney into your grandma's basement—where we been crashing since neither of us can earn a living wage—that put me to the test. I rose to the occasion, just like you said I could.

I got to save you! I never thought I'd be able to do that. You make me a stronger man.

And now, baby, I need you to be strong. 'Cause I feel it, my stomach is growling for brains, and my eyes are getting hazy with rage. I won't be able to make a proper latte for no one anymore.

[*Beat.*]

If you can't do it, I understand. I can go outside, you lock the door behind me, leave me to my fate. Well you might need to drag me, I think my other foot is coming loose and—

. . . oh, you got the gun. That's . . . great. I will always be with you my belov—

[*A SHOT rings out.* DWAYNE *slumps to the floor.*]

Girls Like Us

Jennifer Dickinson

IZZY, 14

Lights come up on a podium inside a church. Next to the podium is an open casket. IZZY, *uncomfortable in her stuffy clothes, stands behind the podium.*

IZZY   I wasn't going to speak today, but I'm so sick of hearing how ladylike Aunt Carla was. Aunt Carla wasn't ladylike. She was fierce. She's the reason I know how to play baseball. She told me once I have the strongest arm of any girl she's seen pitch. After I threw my last no-hitter, my mom took me to Shake Shack for a cherry cone to celebrate. Aunt Carla used to love that place. Unfortunately, my sister went, too. [*Looks for Janine in crowd, then waves.*] Hi, Janine. [IZZY *again addresses the crowd.*] It really sucks when your sister calls you a pig for the way you eat. She and Mom are obsessed with their weight.

Morning at my house goes like this. Mom and Janine high-five after sprinkling one-fourth a teaspoon of brown sugar on their grapefruits, the only sugar they're allowed for the day. Then Janine packs lunch: six carrots and a tablespoon of crunchy almond butter. Mom swears she only eats apples while we're at school, but Janine found a Ziploc of Oreos inside the Bible and now she wants to install security cameras.

Mom, you should know Aunt Carla thought it was ridiculous that you had pictures of Heidi Klum plastered across our refrigerator door. She never believed you were searching for God. She said your God is Heidi Klum.

Last night, when Janine took down those pictures, I thought things were going to change. But then Janine said Mom should have a new thinspiration and handed her a picture. Of Mom. On her wedding day. Some of you were there but I've never seen her in a dress before and her smile seemed real, the way she looks when she eats one-fourth of a devil's food cupcake. She's so tiny you can see her chest bone poking out and Janine pointed to Mom's bone and said: "Banish weakness."

Mom started crying and told Janine to burn the photo. But Janine stuck it in Heidi Klum's old place, right next to my baseball schedule. I said maybe Mom and Janine should break a sweat once in a while. Maybe if their bodies felt stronger they wouldn't be so weak around food. I thought that was pretty genius, but Janine rolled her eyes and said I should go on a diet, too. She said guys will like me if I lose ten pounds. She still doesn't believe that I don't want to get married and have a gazillion kids. [*Imitating Janine.*] *Izzy, you're not a lesbian. You're just scared of letting a boy see you naked.*

But I am a lesbian, everybody. I like girls and I like their bodies. Aunt Carol introduced me to Degas. I love the paintings of the women bathing. Aunt Carla said the Degas women were like us. They have curves. They look healthy.

I was there the day Aunt Carla found out she was sick. You should know she didn't cry. Or freak out. Or anything you'd expect. She made me go outside with her, in the rain, and swim in the river. She raced me to the first rock and she won. She told me she would beat the cancer.

Mom made me look in the casket. For closure, she said. But I don't feel closed. I feel like I've been busted wide open. Aunt Carla doesn't look like the Degas paintings anymore. Her cheeks are grey and hollowed out and someone smeared red lipstick across her mouth. She looks so scary. I tried to wipe the lipstick off, but Janine pulled me away. She said I was being disrespectful. But Aunt Carla hated makeup. She looked beautiful exactly way she was. She told me I did, too.

The girls at school call me fat and ugly. It's a fight not to believe them. But If Aunt Carla were here, I know she'd tell me to keep fighting. She'd promise me I can win.

Hmmm . . .

Benjamin Ridge

J, 18 to 25

J is in his bedroom talking with Andy, a college friend, before they go out to a gay bar. Grungy band posters and broken skateboards surround them.

J We spoke on Grindr and he very obviously didn't like my nose ring. He said so. "Can you take it out?" he asked. No, I fucking can't. We hadn't even met, and he was trying to change me. What time do you want to leave for this gay bar, Andy? Well, I don't like this shirt—I look like an expressionist painting. I want to get there before all the praying Daddies arrive!

Anyway, so me and this guy carried on, flirting and sending pictures. I was too horny to worry about my identities integrity. He opened the door with a quiet voice. "Hmmm," he said. "Hmmm"!!! How rude. He was shorter than I expected. More like Mrs. Doubtfire's face than I expected. So yeah, a dead man in drag. But stocky. Manly. Do you

think this shirt makes me look like John Travolta? No, of
course I don't want to look closeted, but I don't want dudes
trying to piss on me because I'm flaming! Can you even look
bisexual?

We walked to the top flat. He had already dimmed the lights,
wine out and film on. He had done this before. This was only
my second time of thinking with my penis. What was I
supposed to do? I wasn't sure whether to do a backflip or get
out a laminated and clean STI certificate to prove my
worthiness, you know?! Is lube weird in that sort of situation,
or is that just too intense for the first time with a woman?
Pass me another beer, would you?

So we sat on the couch. I asked for water to sober up. His
walk was off-putting. Like he wore small heels. Big arms,
though. I tried to concentrate on the arms. I had drank and
smoked alone to get through the door. The last thing I
wanted to do was to fuck it up by hurling! From the kitchen I
heard, "I don't do this much." [*Pause.*] He'd only taken his
bloody jeans off in the kitchen! Oh God, then he sat next to
me. My body language was horrendous, completely closed off.
I was terrified. He put his hand on my leg and started
rubbing. I was totally freaking out. God damn it, calm down.
He obviously knew what he was doing. Just sit.

I wasn't sure whether to make conversation about the film he
had on. I wasn't even sure we would watch it all the way
through. Was this like that "Netflix and chill" thing that

people keep talking about? Suddenly he said, "I will watch it another time," and closed the laptop. Fuck. He turned and asked me if I like kissing.

I don't know about you, Andy, but bi and gay guys ask this a lot, right? It seems to be all too common a question between men who are about to put their nobs in each others' mouths. I mean, who doesn't like kissing? Do some people who do this have so much shame and self-disgust that they can't even share air? I don't really see the point of not kissing. If I didn't want to kiss, then I may as well stay at home and fuck my hand. again.

We kissed. He tasted like onions. The firmness was arousing. Different. This was only the third time I've kissed a man. The first time was with my mate, you know, Jake, for a dare, and the second time I got totally washing machined. [J *enacts washing machine mouth motion*.] It was different. I liked it. He undid my shirt. Apparently my nose ring was acceptable now. Although, it fucking hurt every time I knocked it. I've only had it pierced a week. Thanks for piercing it for me, by the way. There was something uncomfortably sadomasochistic about me doing it to myself.

We fooled around more. I really hoped no piercing goo would come out. Well, not that part of my body anyway! He kissed my chest. I kissed him more passionately, as if holding a lover's face. I didn't love him, obviously—we'd only just met—but I wanted to feel alive; I'm constantly chasing experience. Anything to make me feel alive, other than breathing. Quick, someone stab me! [J *and Andy laugh.*]

The he said we should lie down. We went to his room. He smelt of the gym, sweaty and sexy. Pure. We were lying on his bed, in our underwear. We took each other out and he placed me in his mouth. Two and half minutes later and I finished. He insisted I do so in his mouth. Whatever dude. More fool you. I smoke, so. A rush of light. I sunk back. I politely said, "That was nice." God.

Then I said that I had to go because my friend was cooking me dinner. This was true. *You* thought I had gone out to get booze! I was only supposed to be an hour. I put my clothes on and walked out. I didn't know what to say, so I said, "Thank you." Dude, I hate myself. Is this what my mom means when she talks about Irish Catholic guilt? I'm not even Catholic. Could it be genetic? We're divorcing you as parents out of shame!

It wasn't that weird that I wouldn't do it again. I'm only human. A horny one at that! I'm gonna have to get hammered before this bar, though. Come on, we're going to be late. I want to get laid tonight; can you check who's online? I fancy Mexican tonight!

When We Were Still Us

Darina Parker

ALLISON, 24 to 37

It is daytime, and ALLISON *and her best friend of 10 years, Elisa (24 to 37 years old), have been traveling on a party bus from Los Angeles to Las Vegas for a mutual friend's wedding.* ALLISON *is fed up with tension-filled silence between the two of them, and she takes an opportunity to reconcile the relationship by following Elisa into the single-person stall of a sketchy gas station bathroom and does her best to clear the air and express what she has been repressing for years.*

ALLISON   Okay, before you freak out, I know we're in this really offensive-smelling bathroom and I know we haven't spoken in over five months, despite us being on a freakin' party bus to freakin' Vegas for the last two hours and forty-seven minutes! I know I'm the last person you want to be in here with, but I've had enough drinks to finally speak up. Two minutes is all I ask. I'm just going to dive right in. I'm an idiot—no, I mean *you're* an idiot—no, what I mean is we're idiots. This isn't how I planned to open. [ALLISON *begins to survey their surroundings.*] This bathroom is throwing me off, Is that? I swear there's blood on the wall! Is that a condom? Why is there a tooth lodged in the wall? No, never mind. I need to focus! We owe it to ourselves and our friends who are about to be joined in holy matrimony to at least clear the air before we get to the wedding and pretend we're okay with the way things are. [ALLISON *refocuses herself.*] Look, all I know is I don't know anything, except, I miss you. Not one day in these last five months has gone by where you haven't been the first thing, the last thing, and the only thing in my thoughts— seriously, I should charge rent. I loathe hauling the hole you made when you left. Nothing is right anymore. I know! I know! You have to pee . . . don't let me stop you. See? This is what I mean—we've been to the bathroom together hundreds of times before. Why is it so awkward now? I don't get it! It's so stupid! Why can't we be the us we were when we were still us? I want—no, *need*—you back. I miss your stupid jokes, I miss your smile, and I miss spending time with you. I don't want to only be able to speak with you because you're trapped in a gas station bathroom that I'm sure is an active crime scene. Seriously, though, we should report this to the manager and get the FBI out here. But first, the point of this valiant declaration is, I only broke things off between us because I was terrified of what we were becoming, of what I was repressing. I have a knack for pushing people away when I feel vulnerable. With you, I was beginning to realize that I. I am utterly in love with you. I realize you're a woman and I'm a woman and this makes me a lesbian. But, Elisa, whenever I see you, I just wanna rub my face all up in you, I mean after you've washed. Of course, I'm missing the point, which is, I'm terrified . . . not because I think there's a severed finger in the corner, but because I realized that I am super lady gay for my best friend and I have been for years, but I was too afraid to accept it. No more fears, no more denial, no more tears, it's time to reconcile. And now I'm speaking in poems. I'm sorry, but I cannot be in here anymore, otherwise spilling my guts will happen literally. [ALLISON *opens the door.*] Uh Elisa, you have your phone, right? Because the bus. the bus is no longer with us. Boy, I am just missing a lot of things these days.

Judy's Guy Friday

Jamison Scala

CYAN DUBOIS, 60s

CYAN DUBOIS, *a driver for Uber, is a man who has seen all that Hollywood has to offer and he'll tell you about it through his curmudgeon filter.*

CYAN DUBOIS   Hi, you must be Jennastin. Welcome to my car. Off to SoulCycle we go. There's Starbright Peppermints if you desire. [CYAN DUBOIS *starts driving.*] Huh. Stars. Oh, I know all about stars. It was 1948. I was seven years old and I was resuscitating my mother on the kitchen floor of our hut. She had choked on the last crust of bread we had. And as her soul left her body, it said, "Cyan, you're destined for greatness. The world is waiting for you, Cyan Dubois." So, there I was. Motherless, alone, and hungry in Tampa. What to do? Become a star. I sold Mother's kidneys to the butcher and boarded a bus for Hollywoodland with seven dollars in my pocket and the crust of bread I ripped out of my dead mother's atrophied throat. That crust lasted me the whole bus ride from Tampa to Los Angeles. Eight days and nights. Put

that in your menorah! I got a long-term motel room at the
Saharan Motel on Sunset. Back then it wasn't frequented by
meth users and transsexuals. The motel was clueless I had no
guardian. I claimed my mother was always indisposed—one of
those schemes like in the movie *Home Alone 2: Lost in New
York*. I digress. I met Judy Garland in 1961 in West
Hollywood. Long before the sexting and homosexual orgies.
We met at an AA meeting on Robertson. Judy was back on
the bottle—no thanks to MGM—and I was looking for
friends. I became her guy Friday and the rest is history.
Weekends at Hearst Castle, yachting with Princess Grace,
and covering up indiscretions for the Kennedys. All of them,
including Jackie! When Judy died she left it all to the kids:
Liza, Lorna, and that twink, Joey. I guess sneaking into the
women's room of Canter's Deli at four a.m. to help change
your friend's soiled panties isn't worth what it used to be. So I
know all about stars. [*There's a beat, and* CYAN DUBOIS *pulls
over.*] Speaking of which, I hope you'll rate me 5 stars. Uber's
been up my ass to get up my driver rating. [*He presses door
unlock button.*] The doors are unlocked!

If Only

Tiffany E. Babb

JOAN/JOHN, 21 to 27

JOAN/JOHN *is sitting at a lonely bar speaking to a member of the clergy.*

JOAN/JOHN   Well, that was an adventure of sorts. This whole night, really. I don't know whether or not it's this particular bar, but I don't think I've ever been hit on by the wrong gender so much in one day. Thank you, dearly, for rescuing me from the hordes of . . . suitors.

[*Beat.*]

Don't you ever feel like you wish that people just knew that you were queer?

[*Beat.*]

I mean, sans wearing a T-shirt or having to wear a pin or playing into queer coding or something. Like if there was just a way of divining people's sexuality right when you meet

them. Imagine how useful that would be, even from, you
know, the other side's point of view.

[*Beat.*]

Like some sort of invisible sign which says, "Yo! I'm totally
not into dudes," or "Hey! I swing both ways," or "Nope, no
romance for me."

[*Beat.*]

It would also fix the huge annoyance in life, which is coming
out. I think what people usually don't get is that coming out
isn't just a one-step process. Tell everyone you know and see
who sticks around afterwards. And yes, people understand
that coming out sucks sometimes. But what people don't get is
that it never ends. Every time you go to a new place, get a
new job, meet new people. You always have to find the "right
time" to tell them that you're not straight. I don't know if it's
like this for everybody, but when I'm hanging out with
someone who doesn't know about my sexuality, I kind of feel
like I'm hiding it. Even when I'm not.

[*Beat.*]

This whole thing obviously wouldn't be as big of a problem if
in most peoples' minds "heterosexual" wasn't the default. But
since it is, you have to squeeze the telling in between
introducing yourself to a stranger at the bar and, you know,

becoming best pals . . . I'm [JOAN/JOHN], by the way. I've never met a member of the clergy before.

[*Beat.*]

God. So what was my point again? Oh yeah, sorry. I'm queer! Yes, I know it's kind of weird that I'm telling you right now because we met, like, five minutes ago, when you were saving me from that [*guy/girl*]. But hey! Now you know. I am absolutely not at all interested in [*men/women*].

[*Beat.*]

And since you know, now, that I'm queer . . . Is it weird for me to ask you whether or not you're allowed to date? I know some churches have different rules. And if you *are* allowed to date, are you straight? Because if not . . . how about a drink?

The *Talk*

Leah Mann

DWAYNE, 40s to 50s

DWAYNE *has gone into the bedroom of his tween daughter to talk with her. He nervously approaches her.*

DWAYNE   Sweetie, sit down. We have to talk.

[*Beat.*]

Yes, we have to. No, you're not in trouble. It's not a bad talk.

Um . . . yes, it is an awkward talk. But I hope that we can be open and honest with each other and it won't be too awkward.

YES. Now. It has to happen now . . . . Because I'm ready and you're not doing anything and I don't want to wait any longer. Remember what I told you about procrastination?

[*Beat.*]

It's bad.

[*Beat.*]

You don't have to say anything. Just listen.

[*Beat.*]

Give me your phone.

[*Beat.*]

Thank you.

[*Beat.*]

No, you can't turn on the TV. Just sit down and we'll get this over with, okay?

[*Beat.*]

Okay. So . . . as you may have noticed, you are becoming a woman and with that comes changes. Big changes that you've learned a bit about—I hope—in health class.

[*Beat.*]

Yup, like those. Exactly. I want you to know that your father and I are here for you and we will answer any questions you have. Now, we know that you recently got your . . . your . . .

[*Beat.*]

Your Period.

We know because the school nurse called us.

Do you have any questions? We bought you some tampons and pads and a Diva Cup and adult diapers. Not that you're incontinent—that means you pee yourself—but we just wanted you to have all the options.

We love you so much and you're our little girl and . . . I mean . . . Are you okay? Really, God, I can't imagine how scared you have been, blood flowing out of your . . .

[*Shudders.*]

Was it messy? I hate blood.

[*Beat.*]

How do you use a tampon . . . ? That's a great question. I'm pretty sure you put it in your—um, you know—your vagina.

[*Beat.*]

Where, exactly? Um . . . The vagina hole? Isn't there just one? I haven't actually encountered one personally. I guess technically my mother's, but I don't remember any of the anatomical details. Do you have a separate pee hole? I should have done more research on this. There's a diagram in the tampon box, if you want. Obviously pads are easier and if you're more comfortable with that for now, that's fine. No one will know.

[*Beat.*]

My God, what DO you do during swim class? I never thought
about it. Shit, I can call your Aunt Jenn. Let's put that on the
TBD list.

[*Beat.*]

The cup? I think it's the same as a tampon, only you wash it
and reuse it . . . I'm sure it's sanitary or it wouldn't be FDA
approved. It's better for the environment. I know how
important that is to you. [*Beat.*] I don't know how big. I mean,
we can open the box and see how big the cup is, but I don't
know big your . . . you know . . . how could I know that? You
must have a rough idea . . .

This is getting . . . detailed.

[*Beat.*]

Um . . . . ugh. Okay, I could give you a mirror. They say that's
a very healthy way to learn about yourself. Not that I've ever,
I mean, my bits are all just hanging out there. No mirror
necessary . . . ha ha ha haaaaaa . . . .

[*Beat.*]

Sorry. That was inappropriate. Let's move on.

I know you'll have symptoms. Like, uh, cramps and aches and
cravings and you might get moody . . .

. . . I'm not saying you ARE moody, I'm saying you could, in the future, experience mood swings as a hormonal side effect of becoming a woman. And I want you to know that your father and I are sympathetic to that.

[*Beat.*]

Of course we don't know what it's LIKE, we don't have ovaries or fallopian tubes or uteruses—uteri? But we love you and we also have emotions and we both know what it's like to have a tough time and if you ever need a little extra space or affection because of that time, just let us know. The important thing is that we communicate.

[*Beat.*]

Do you need a bra? Boobs and periods go together, right? That's my understanding.

[*Beat.*]

Well, I don't know! Do I look like I have boobs? God, please tell me I'm not that fat. Your father is right. I have to watch my snacking. You don't have to wear a bra if you don't want to, but if you do want to, we can go shopping for one. And razors. If you want. You can use ours, of course. You should. If you want to! You don't have to. Hairy armpits are completely natural. You can even dye them if you want! People do that now. Either way, if you do shave don't spend the extra money on a "girl" razor. They call it pink-washing—

they jack up the price on the same exact product just because it's for women. That's gender discrimination and we'll have no part in it. Unless you like pink, in which case money is no object.

[*Beat.*]

The take-away here is that we love you, and are here for you, and whatever you need in the becoming a woman/menstruation area, we want to give you.

Do you have any questions about boys? I can help there. I'm an expert on boys. Not that you have to like boys. Just logistically, I can be more help there . . .

[*Beat.*]

No? Just the tampons.

[*Beat.*]

I better get that diagram.

Transition

Alessandra Rizzotti

AMANDA, 18

AMANDA *is standing at the high school lockers talking with her friend Sarah after the last bell.*

AMANDA   Sarah, you know how we're prepping for nationals this year? I figured I didn't want to compete with a duet with you like last year. Don't get me wrong, I love working with you. I just want to end high school on a big note.

[*Beat.*]

Can you listen? Seriously. Don't get all hissy fitty on me. I've been working on a play about a guy who doesn't want to come out to his parents. It's sweet. Sensual. Pretty PG. Almost like *Blossom* meets *Glee*. Remember the floating bag in *American Beauty*? It's like the tone of that.

[*Beat.*]

No, Sarah—I'm not gay. I just think this play is probably the easiest way to express myself to drama club this year. Because, I dunno. There's no other way to talk about this. Sarah, I want to tell you something. Can you listen?

[*Beat.*]

Why are you so excited? What I'm about to tell you might weird you out and I'm nervous. Stop smiling. Okay. Here goes. I always knew I liked dressing up in women's clothes since I was two years old, but I'm starting to realize that that's not gay . . . that's something else. I've been looking it up on Google and I am realizing that I really identify as a woman. OMG. Can you listen? Because I want you to be the first person I told. You really helped me that one time when you and I were putting on makeup for fun, and I just realized in that moment how natural and good that felt. It felt like myself. Because when I put on skater shorts and baggy shirts, I feel like I'm outside my skin.

[*Beat.*]

Sarah, no, you can't tell anyone. I sorta need to do this on my own. I was thinking that I could do it at the end of the play. My mom and dad don't know. Honestly, they would probably be fine with it. I found heels in my dad's car once, so either he is having an affair or he dresses up like a woman, too. And as for my mom, she knows I wear her lipstick in my room and dance to Diana Ross. I mean, she sometimes wants to join. So it's no big deal on my family end. I just sorta want to be able to come out to all the kids at school in a really dignified sorta way.

[*Beat.*]

Why? Because it would be freeing. I don't want to start my life as a whole new person in college. I want to be the person I've always wanted to be, starting now. Why can't you understand that?

[*Beat.*]

We're best friends, Sarah. I don't like you that way. Shut up. You didn't think I liked you, did you? We're soul mates. That's a different kind of love. OMG. Are you serious? My sexuality is fluid. I like boys and girls, just not you. I swear I didn't mean to hurt you this way. Sarah, I thought we were so close because we were just best friends. No! I thought you wanted to wait till marriage to kiss and have sex—not for ME. Ah! This is so confusing. I didn't mean to confuse you.

[*Beat.*]

I love you, but not in a sexual way. How did this become about us and not me? You always do that. Can't you listen for once? Can't you hear me out? Are we not going to be friends anymore? OMG. I thought you were a Christian liberal. One day when the world isn't so bigoted, I'll be able to be myself.

[*Beat.*]

What? I thought you were mad. Well I'm not in love back.
I'm sorry. This conversation just made me asexual.

Uber Uber

Lisa Gopman

MARCUS BLACK, 28

MARCUS BLACK *is in an Uber heading into New York City. He is talking to his Uber driver, Mateo.*

MARCUS BLACK   Hi! Are you Mateo? Great. I know some Uber drivers aren't really into talking, but I'm just so excited! I'm here to make my dreams come true!!

I'm really in N-Y-C. Wow. I guess I've always just thought about things a little differently, you know. Some call me a drama queen. I'm okay with "dramatic," but I'm way too young to be considered a queen. I look good.

I'm going to take over this city, Mateo. I have survival skills. I guess you could say I have creative ways of solving problems. Like last month, when I was struggling in the middle of a CRISIS. I was housesitting for my bestie—he is, by the way, a semifamous actor. Like Taystee-from-*Orange-Is-the-New-Black* famous. Anywho, I had a sitch with my car and ended up being STRANDED in the HOLLYWOOD HILLS with absolutely no food. So there's only one thing I could do. I quickly sent out a 911 group text to all my besties. Thank G-d most people are at my beck and call and got back to me immediately. I began to spread the word: "Everyone. Get over here, EMERGENCY POTLUCK." Many of my friends showed up with life's essentials. Sushi and Tito's Vodka. Thank G-d. Crisis averted. One of my fruit flies was a little mad, though, because she forgot how inventive I can be and left work thinking I was in like life or death danger. Don't worry, Mateo. It was nothing some Jello shots and a Beyoncé dance party couldn't save.

Speaking of Beyoncé, Bey is EVERYTHING to me. P.S. Do you have any idea where she lives? I would die if I met her. You know how most people put an angel on top of their Christmas tree? Well, every year I put a Beyoncé angel on top of my tree. Because there is no one more fierce, more glorious, more on point than Bey. More than a few times, I've left the room at a party and danced back in to "Single Ladies" or "Drunk in Love" in full Beyoncé attire. Oh, and it doesn't matter if I am at someone else's house. I will find something that the Queen would wear in an emergency.

FYI—I also LOVE a chance for a good dance routine. I bet you know some dance moves, Mateo. My best showcase opportunity is awards shows. Obvi I am going to get a Tony someday. So I like to scope out my competition and watch

every single dance moment. My favorite was the year of
Chicago the movie. Magical dance numbers were everywhere.
Especially at the Oscars. My heart was racing with glee when
"All That Jazz" started. I forgot that I was yet again housesitting for a star. I normally drop names, but this time I'll just
hint and say technically he came in second place on *Idol* his
season, but I think we can all agree he was the real winner.
You know who I'm talking about! Anywho, as I began to
channel Fosse with every part of my being, my kicks got
higher and higher. I forgot about all my friends in the room.
That's when my kicks got bigger and more fantastic and with
one giant kick I kicked an entire table of barbecue sauce and
chicken wings into the air. Out of the corner of my eye I saw
it sprawl all over the stark white curtains and the white rug
and all over the face of my girl Jalisa. But if I live by one
motto, it's "the show must go on." So I kept kicking and jazz
handing and smiling until the very last note. I absolutely
killed it. Speaking of, here we are. Broadway!! This is so
amazing! My college roommate said I should meet him here
because our new apartment is really close. Look at these
marquees!! That's going to be me some day. Five stars for you,
Mateo. Thank you for all your love and inspiration on my
first day in N-Y-C. And Broadway—you better be ready for
me, because I am SO ready for you!

Meat Is Murder

Corrine Glazer

RACQUEL, 21

RACQUEL *is a college senior majoring in humanities. She has an enchanting smile and a sheltered, girl-next-door appeal . . . until she opens up and her neurosis comes out. In this monologue, she's in an on-campus bar drinking and flirting with a male classmate. They are swapping girlfriend stories.*

RACQUEL   I met my first girlfriend at a Meat Is Murder protest in the campus dining hall. She took my breath away. We didn't talk much the first two days. Okay, I was far too intimidated to formulate words. But on the third day, we chatted so hard, I'm not sure when it became just the two of us standing in the middle of the dining hall. That's when it happened. Her eyes sparkled and my heart raced as her porcelain skin, chiseled cheeks, and plush lips fast approached mine. I swallowed the loudest swallow in the history of the Universe. But that kiss . . . I wanted to be chained forever to the anchor tattoo on the inside of her wrist. When it was over, I could barely speak, so when she asked me over to her

off-campus apartment, I just nodded my head. I was so
nervous. I mean, she was a senior and I was a freshman. I had
never even spent the night out of my dorm. And this was a
lesbian! She led me into her place and then she went to use
her bathroom. I wasn't sure what to do with myself, so I sat
on her couch. My eyes scanned the room from the windows
on the left, past her bookshelf, past her TV, and into the
kitchen to the right. I stared at her refrigerator door. [*Beat.*] It
stared back at me. I didn't blink for what felt like eternity. I
guess it had only been a few seconds, but those seconds felt
like hours passing. I looked back towards the bathroom. She
wasn't coming out yet. I looked back at the fridge. And again
back at the bathroom. I don't know what was taking her so
long! I looked back at the fridge door. I could hear the
creaking sound it makes when it opens and I could see the
light inside coming on. [*Beat.*] I have a disorder. Every time I
enter someone's house, I have to see what they have to eat. I
have to check inside cabinets and pantries and fridges and
freezers. [*Beat.*] I try controlling my impulse. I look back at
the bathroom. No movement yet. No shadows of feet
blocking light at the bottom of the door. I look back at the
fridge. I can see the light inside burning so bright it's flooding
out the cracks of the door. I have to check that her light isn't
stuck on. It could be heating up her food. It could be melting
the plastic! Before I know it, I'm in the kitchen, my arm
outstretched with my hand gripping the handle. One quick
look. I'm barely half a sigh of euphoria in, when her
disorganization disrupts my breath. No turning back now. I'm

frantically twisting her labels to face out when I notice she has
a lot of peanut butter. Like shop-at-Costco a lot. But she lives
alone. And doesn't she know Jif is not the kind of peanut
butter that needs to be refrigerated? She's ruining its
spreadability! Unless she doesn't spread it and just eats it by
the spoonful. That could be why she's taking so long in the
bathroom; peanuts are very constipating. If that's the issue,
that affords me time to organize her yogurts. She has them on
all different shelves! I take them out and arrange them by
flavor. No way she can eat this much yogurt before their
expiration. Unless she has a yeast infection. Now that may be
why she is taking so long in the bathroom. And if she has a
yeast infection, I can't go down on her. I can get yeast in my
mouth, right? I'm thinking I should go, but I can't help but
wonder what else she's hiding. I unload her fridge from the
top shelf down. Her produce is haphazardly stuffed
everywhere and not stored in the crisper drawers! Everyone
knows one side is for fruit and the other side for veggies. I
open up a crisper drawer and find she's packing meat. What
happened to Meat Is Murder? Who did I go home with?! I
can't stop myself. I pull out bacon, steak, chicken breasts. I'm
sweating. If this stuff isn't in her freezer, she plans on eating
all of it this week! I'm getting sick. I should have never put my
hands in her drawers! I've got all that meat in one hand as I
reach in with my other and pull out a phallic package of
truffled salami. Marin's concerned voice scares the crap out of
me and I drop all the meat at my feet. Right then I notice I
have all of her food, from the yogurt to the peanut butter,

even her exposed produce, all over the unsanitary floor. I
slowly turn my head, expecting to see some . . . I don't know,
grotesque creature, some liar, but all I see is Marin. Beautiful,
handsome Marin with a soft, golden glow around her. And all
I want to do is slam into her body like a meat tenderizer and
sink my teeth into her neck like a filet mignon.

Pray the Gay Away

Jamison Scala

BILL, 40s

BILL *is as gay as the day is long, but straight as an arrow for God.*

BILL I want to thank you all for joining me and Joyce tonight
in our home. It's so lovely to have our friends congregating in
our formal living room again, just like the old days. But we
didn't invite you here just for my world-famous seven-layer
dirt pudding. Although, that's enough of an excuse, right?!
Ha-ha. Over the past month, I'm sure you noticed one less
tenor belting away in the Sunday morning church choir and
that tenor would be moi. I had to go away for a bit. You may
have heard I was a homosexual, but it looks like God had
another plan for me. Thanks to prayer and the kind people at
the Federalsburg Abomination Group—also known as
FAG—I am now as straight as the spine on a Broadway
playbill. Over the past month, me and ten other handsome
but misguided men, POUNDED the good book into our
souls, THRUSTED ourselves into counseling, and were
DRIPPING WET with salvation from electroshock therapy.

And just like Elizabeth Smart, I have been saved, too. I'm so happy to be back home with my loyal wife, Joyce, so we can get back to our true loves: God, friends, and Danish cooking classes. Not to mention the joy of good old-fashioned male-female intimacy, as God intended. I'm sure I speak for the both of us when I say we can't wait to get all our friends out of here so we can be intimate! I jest, I jest. Now, it may be the electroshock therapy talking, but doesn't Frank eating that sausage make him look like he's gobbling down my dick?

Three's a Crowd

Leah Mann

CASSIE, 20s to 30s

CASSIE *is pretty, chatty, and completely self-involved. It is evening, and she is meeting a first date at a bar. She is sitting at the bar, sipping a beer. She waves as her date enters, and she pats the seat next to her.*

CASSIE   Hi! You must be Mia! It's so nice to meet you. Wow, you're even prettier than your picture. I love your glasses. Sexy. Sit, what do you want to drink?

[*Beat.*]

I'm having the hef—it's good. Want to try it?

[*Beat.*]

Right? So good!

Have you been on a lot of these?

[*Beat.*]

Right?! So awkward, but I've met some nice people and some not-so-nice people and, you know, it's all just people! Ha-ha-ha.

[*Beat.*]

What should you know about me? I grew up in North Carolina, college in Florida, came here for a girl about eight years ago and just stayed. I'm into all the usual: hiking, yoga, whatever . . . Not a big reader, but I've been keeping a blog of my dating adventures that gets, like, a ton of views. Maybe I shouldn't tell you that! Ha-ha. It's all totally anonymous, though, so don't worry. And if you're boring, then there's nothing to worry about because I won't have anything to say.

[*Beat.*]

I hope you're not boring. I HATE boring. Oh my God, this beer is giving me life right now. I'm going to have to run it off tomorrow, but it's worth it, right?

[*Beat.*]

Oh man, work? So many things—I tutor and babysit; like I said, I write . . . but the blog doesn't bring in much money. I want to start a vlog. Some of those YouTube people make six figures! It's insane. I'm pretty charismatic and relatable, so I think I could do it. It'd be about, like, you know, dating tips and healthy eating and maybe do-it-yourself stuff. I get a lot of clothes from the thrift store and up-cycle them, which I think people would be into. So yeah, that's how I get by.

[*Beat.*]

It's cool, though, because Brian makes bank, so if I have a slow month with tutoring it's all good . . . did you meet Brian?

[*Beat.*]

He's playing foosball. Hold on—BRIAN! BRIIAAANN!!!

[*Beat.*]

This is Brian, my boyfriend. Brian, this is Mia.

[*Beat.*]

Oh God! The look on your face. You're hilarious. Don't worry, we're not like into threesomes or anything. We're probably going to break up eventually anyways, because he's kind of fratty for me and I drive him crazy. It's all good, though, because I am so GRATEFUL for the friendship we do have and the memories we've created. I'm super blessed.

[*Beat.*]

I don't think it's weird that he's here. He's still my best friend. Well, he's still my boyfriend. I mean, we still have sex, like, all the time. But for me, being on dates is a safety issue. You know? People are crazy and I've had some total creeps get stalky and stuff.

He's also the driver—so I can drink, because I get nervous around new people . . . I LOVE new people—like meeting new souls and connecting is the most amazing thing in the world—but I'm also a little shy, and being able to have a drink or two helps open me up and allow new things to come into my heart.

Like you.

[*Beat.*]

I'd consider myself an omnisexual. Anyone can turn me on; it's really about their soul and inner beauty. I think every being has a unique and gorgeous light inside them, and if I connect with that, then I'm in. Brian has a special soul, which is why we still have so much sex. The stuff about who has a penis or tits or whatever is irrelevant to me. Anyone can have tits! It doesn't make you hot or ugly or a woman or anything. They're just tits, right?

[*Beat.*]

You're totally gay? Wow! That's hardcore. I mean, I just don't think I could ever commit to just one sex. Have you ever been with a guy?

[*Beat.*]

Never!?! Don't you feel like you're limiting yourself? I believe it's really important not to limit yourself in life. You never know what's behind any given door. I had this one boyfriend, but he was transgender. He grew up female but transitioned in college, and so we had all those girl experiences from childhood in common but totally different perspectives and he just opened my eyes up to the world.

You should really think about expanding your horizons. Maybe you should have a threesome. It's important to try new things.

You're so tense—God, relax. I'm sorry if I'm "not what you expected," but Jesus—it's twenty sixteen, right? I'm sure Brian would be down. He's a very considerate and gentle person in bed. Aren't you, babe?

[*Beat.*]

Look, it's getting late. It was nice to meet you, but I don't think this is a good fit. You're just so quiet and repressed. No offense, it's just not my vibe. I mean, we've been talking for how long and I don't know anything about you except that you aren't into penises. We're going to go.

Good luck.

Contributors

ALISHA GADDIS is a Latin Grammy and Emmy Award–winning performer and actress, humorist, writer, and producer based in Los Angeles. She is a graduate of New York University's Tisch School of the Arts and the University of Sydney, Australia.

Alisha's first book, *Women's Comedic Monologues That Are Actually Funny*, was published by Applause Books in 2014. Subsequently, she signed on with Applause Books to release five more books in this series, which includes the book you are currently holding in your hands. Her columns have appeared in College Candy, Comediva, *GOOD* magazine, and Thought Catalog. Alisha is the founder and head writer of Say Something Funny . . . B*tch!—the nationally acclaimed all-female online magazine. The highly irreverent Messenger Card line that she cofounded and writes for is sold in boutiques nationally.

Alisha currently stars in the TV show she cocreated and executive-produced, *Lishy Lou and Lucky Too*, as part of the Emmy Award–winning children's series *The Friday Zone* on PBS/PBS KIDS.

Alongside her husband, Lucky Diaz, she is the cofounder and performer for Latin Grammy Award–winning Lucky Diaz and the Family Jam Band. Their children's music has topped the charts at Sirius XM and is *People* magazine's No. 1 album of the year—playing Los Angeles Festival of Books, Target Stage, the Smithsonian, the Getty Museum, Madison Square Park, Legoland, New York City's Symphony Space, and more. Their song "Falling" has been used in Coca-Cola's summer national ad campaign.

As a stand-up comic and improviser, Alisha has headlined the nation at the World Famous Comedy Store and the New York Comedy Club, and has been named one of the funniest upcoming female comics by *Entertainment Weekly*. As a performer, she has appeared on Broadway; has performed at the Sydney Opera House, Second City Hollywood, Improv Olympic West, Upright Citizens Brigade, and the Comedy Central Stage; and has toured with her acclaimed solo shows *Step-Parenting: The Last Four Letter Word* and *The Search for Something Grand*. She has also appeared on MTV, CBS, CNN, Univision, NBC, and A&E, and has voiced many national campaigns. Alisha is a proud SAG-AFTRA, NARAS, LARAS, and AEA member.

She loves her husband the most.

Find out more about Alisha at alishagaddis.com.

TIFFANY E. BABB is a Los Angeles–based writer and book hoarder. She recently received her comparative literature degree at the University of Southern California. Tiffany enjoys reading novels, poetry, and comics. Some of her favorite writers include John le Carré, W. H. Auden, Emily Dickinson, and Jorge Luis Borges. When she isn't reading or writing, Tiffany likes to attend comic book conventions, eat brunch, and think about impending doom (usually at separate times). She can be reached at *tiffanyebabb.com*.

KAYLA CAGAN likes to write for all kinds of performers and friends in the theater. She is also a young-adult novelist. She lives happily with her husband and dog in Los Angeles.

JENNIFER DICKINSON received her BA from Hollins University. Her short fiction has appeared in *Blackbird, Other Voices, Word Riot*, and *Mason's Road*. She is the recipient of a Hedgebrook residency and a grant from the Money for Women/Barbara Deming Memorial Fund. She lives in Los Angeles, where she runs a women's writing workshop, Chapter OneWorkshop.com. She is currently working on a novel, a Cain and Abel thriller, for high school girls.

LIBBY DOYNE is a writer and comedian living in Los Angeles. She has a degree in geography from the University of Colorado and is a graduate of The Second City Hollywood and the Up-right Citizens Brigade training centers. She is the proud recipient of the UCLA Writers' Extension Program Scholarship for TV Writing as well as the Thomas Angel Foundation Scholarship for funny women. She lived in a remote village in Nepal for two years before moving to Hollywood. The walls of her apartment are lined with artwork inspired by her one true muse, a pit bull named Hank. She tweets *@libbydoyne*.

TYLER GILLESPIE's writing and reporting have been featured in the *New Yorker, Rolling Stone*, and *The Guardian*, and on Salon and public radio. He's a coeditor of the humor collection *The Awkward Phase* (Skyhorse Publishing, 2016) and a graduate of The Second City Writing Program. He's also the palest Floridian you'll ever meet. Find him on Twitter *@TylerMTG*.

JOSH GINSBURG is a Brooklyn-based playwright and screenwriter. He received his masters in dramatic writing from Carnegie Mellon University in Pittsburgh, PA. His plays have won multiple awards at the Kennedy Center in Washington, DC, and have been performed across the country. His screenplay *Finding Tom Harvey* won the Alfred P. Sloan Screenwriting competition in 2014. You can follow his rarely updated Twitter *@JoshGinsburg*.

JESSICA GLASSBERG is a comedy writer and stand-up comedian. For ten years, she was the head writer on *The Jerry Lewis MDA Telethon* and performed stand-up on the nationally syndicated show five times. She has also written for *Zeke and Luther* on Disney XD, "A Hollywood Christmas at The Grove" for *Extra*, and The Screen Actors Guild Awards (where her jokes were highlighted on E!'s *The Soup*, EntertainmentWeekly.com, and Hollywood.com). Additionally, Glassberg was a featured performer on *The History of the Joke with Lewis Black* on the History Channel. In addition to her monologue that appears in this compilation, Jessica's monologues have also been published in the books *Women's Comedic Monologues That Are Actually Funny*, *Men's Comedic Monologues That Are Actually Funny*, *Teen Boys' Comedic Monologues That Are Actually Funny*, and *Teen Girls' Comedic Monologues That Are Actually Funny*. Jessica is also a prolific digital writer, with her work featured on HelloGiggles. com, Reductress.com, HotMomsClub.com, Kveller.com, Absrd COMEDY.com, attn.com, and Torquemag.io. She has her own blog The Journey of Jessica: Comic Adventures, Misadventures and Misteradventures (with Little Moo) at *https://jessicaglassberg. wordpress.com*. For upcoming shows, clips, and writing samples, check out *www.jessicaglassberg.com* and follow her on Twitter *@JGlassberg*.

CORRINE GLAZER is an actress, writer, and producer for stage, TV, film, and commercials in New York and Los Angeles. She authored (and laughably illustrated) THE CASE OF THE MISSING MITTENS in second grade, prompting her dad's wisdom, "One day you'll realize your true calling to be a writer." During her senior year at Sachem High School, her Journalism teacher submitted her essay "Albert Einstein: Man of the Century" and *Time* Education Program published it in December of 1999, leading then–Executive Editor Bennett Singer to offer Corrine an internship. She turned it down in pursuit of acting. Corrine is an alumna of Presidential Classroom, where she fell in love with wearing suits, but she mostly wore yoga pants in BFA Musical Theatre at Emerson College in Boston, while earning her BFA in drama from NYU Tisch, and training in Russia and at The Groundlings. She still wears suits while managing High Profile Hollywood Events. She snuggles animals to her face despite allergies, belts out made-up songs in the shower, and voices wacky characters to entertain herself. Her superhuman power is making desserts disappear. Find out more about her at *http://resumes.actorsaccess.com/corrineglazer* and follow her upbeat, awkward, and disastrous fumbles through the world on Twitter and Instagram *@IBeGlazin*.

MIKE GLAZER is a comedy writer in Los Angeles. He's written for truTV and CBS, as well as Funny or Die. He was a cast member on Food Network's reality TV cooking competition *Worst Cooks in America*, where he won third place. Now, he no longer burns down his kitchen! His tweets have been featured on Mandatory, BuzzFeed, Someecards, News.com.Au, and he was *Playboy*'s No. 10 Funniest Twitter Account of 2014. He'd like to thank his incredible girlfriend and costume designer, Lindsay Monahan, for being a dream come true. He'd also like to thank his cool family—cool mom Wendi, cool dad Steve, and cool bro Matt—for being the greatest family he could ever ask for. More than anything, Mike hopes you use his monologue, it gets you the job, and you shine like a star! If you like weird jokes, follow him on Twitter *@GlazerBooHooHoo*.

LISA GOPMAN grew up in Cincinnati, OH, and shortly after her eighteenth birthday, headed to L.A. and the USC School of Dramatic Arts. She developed her own humorous college magazine column called "Sketchy Girl" while attending USC. Between her writing and her family motto "Nothing comes easy for Gopmans," she was encouraged by her professors and friends to take her true-life wackiness onto the stand-up stage. She has performed on Comedy Central's *Premium Blend*; she previously won Comedy Central's *Laugh Riots*; she was a featured comedian on MTV's *The Mandy Show*: and she performed in *Just for Laughs*, at the *Boston Comedy Festival*, and in Comedy Central's *Get Up, Stand Up* in Jamaica. Lisa continues to be passionate about writing, stand-up, and acting. She recently cofounded Oh My Ribs! Entertainment with her husband, Matthew, in Hollywood, where she currently produces and hosts a Friday night stand-up show. Lisa is constantly inspired by and grateful for all her supportive friends and family, her dad Arnie, and her amazing husband, Matthew. Special thanks to CB for being her monologue muse. For more info on Lisa's life in comedy, check out *www.lisagopman.com* and *www.ohmyribs.com* and follow her on Twitter *@LisaGopman*.

MOLL GREEN lives in Vancouver and Los Angeles. She writes comics, screenplays, poetry, and lots of other stuff, and her work has most recently appeared in *The 27 Club: A Comic Anthology*, *Skyd magazine*, *PopOptiq*, *Graphic Policy*, and *The Rainbow Hub*. Tweet your sweet nothings *@MadMollGreen*.

KATE HUFFMAN is an actor, writer, and comedian originally from Indianapolis, IN, who currently resides in Los Angeles. She actively works in film (*Exit Plan*), television (*Fresh Off the Boat, Castle*) and theater (Geffen Playhouse, Road Theatre Company, Elephant Theatre Company) in addition to writing, producing, and acting in shorts and web series. Her work in the Elephant Theatre Company's production of *100 Saints You Should Know* won her an Los Angeles Weekly Theatre Award and a nomination for a Los Angeles Drama Critics' Circle Award.

In the comedy realm, Kate performs sketch and improv at the Upright Citizens Brigade Theatre and improv comedy theater iO West. She earned her BFA in acting at the University of Miami, and generally speaking, thinks humans are pretty great.

JP KARLIAK is a voice-over artist, writer, solo performer, and snappy dresser who hails from the "Electric City" Scranton, PA. His voice has fallen out of the mouths of Marvel heroes and villains, a werewolf nemesis of the *Skylanders*, and the self-proclaimed supergenius Wile E. Coyote, among others. On screen, he planned a fancy party for Sarah Michelle Gellar and delivered singing telegrams to *The Real Husbands of Hollywood*. A graduate of the USC School of Theatre, iO West, and Second City Training Center, he has written numerous short films and plays produced in locales around the country. His full-length solo show, *Donna/Madonna*, has garnered awards at the United Solo, New York International Fringe and San Francisco Fringe Festivals. He can always be found at fancy chocolate boutiques or on his website, *jpkarliak.com*.

NINA KI graduated from New York University's Tisch School of the Arts with a Bachelor of Fine Arts in dramatic writing. Her plays have been read and produced in Theatre InspiraTO's ten-minute play festival, Another Country Productions' SLAMBoston and SLAMBoston Uncensored, Kennedy Center American College Theater Festival, Mixed Phoenix Theater Company's Annual Fall Reading Series, and City Theatre of Independence Playwrights Festival. Her poetry has previously been published in *Relationships and Other Stuff*, as well as the *Getting Bi* poetry anthology. Nina Ki is the cofounder of Pearl Girls Productions, and through this independent production group she is producer and writer of an Asian American web series called *That's What She Said*. To contact her, find her on Facebook at *www.facebook.com/ninakiwrites*.

CATHY LEWIS has earned the respect and admiration from international audiences as well as fellow comedians for her stellar humor and philanthropic endeavors. A lifelong survivor of tetralogy of Fallot, a congenital heart condition, Lewis has been a major contributor to the Adult Congenital Heart Association. Being a survivor, Cathy understands firsthand how the support from many organizations can make a difference. It is said that laughter is the best medicine and as a result Lewis founded Big Heart Productions, an organization dedicated to helping charities through comedic benefits and fund-raisers. Lewis has collaborated with the Adult Congenital Heart Association in partnership UCLA, the Make-A-Wish Foundation, Crippled Children's Society, and the Community Alliance for the Blind. Cathy has worked alongside many comedians such as Chris Rock, Damon Wayans, Bill Maher, Margret Cho, and Kevin Pollack to raise not only awareness but also donations for charity. Since her start Cathy has performed at legendary venues such as the Laugh Factory in Hollywood, the Punch Line in San Francisco, and the World Famous Comedy Store on Sunset Strip, where she has been a staple since owner Mitzy Shore discovered her in 1991. Cathy's trajectory has ranged from voice-overs in Nickelodeon's cartoon *Teapot* and ADA Sport's *Pussy Slapping!* to TV appearances on Logo's *One Night Stand Up*, BET's *ComicView*, NBC's *Last Comic Standing* and *The Jenny Jones Show*. She has produced the long-time running live shows Cathy Lewis & Friends, Sheezz Funny, and The Nappy Fro Show atthe world famous Comedy Store. Follow her on Twitter @*cathylewiscomic*.

LEAH MANN grew up in Washington, DC, and graduated from Brown University in 2003. Since moving to Los Angeles in 2004, she has written several screenplays, television specs, and short stories, and one novel that no one will ever see. Her short story "Going Solo" was published alongside work by prominent authors such as Neil Gaiman and Ray Bradbury in the horror anthology *Psychos: Serial Killers, Depraved Madmen, and the Criminally Insane*. She is delighted to have a number of monologues included in the *Comedic Monologues That Are Actually Funny* collections for *Men, Teen Boys, Teen Girls, Kids, and LGBTQ*. Leah currently works as a set decorator and property master. She digs crosswords, her garden (get it . . . "digs" her garden . . .), cuddling with her dog, and reading books. Find out more about her at *www.leahmann.com*.

DARINA PARKER Here's a story about me that will give you a great idea about who I am. I've lived in New York City and now live in Los Angeles, and am originally from Michigan, where I grew up playing basketball. I'm obsessed with TED Talks. I love being outdoors, playing kickball, and most of all, enjoying the moment. One of my bravest moments occurred in April of 2015. Headed home after winning my best kickball game of our season. At the time I didn't have a car and my phone had no charge, so I needed to take the metro. A friend dropped me off at the station in North Hollywood just in time for the last train before it stopped running for the night. Knowing such information I hastily sprinted down the stairs. Halfway down I slipped and broke my ankle. I panicked, but was very determined to make it home. I punched the bone back in, twice, got on the train, and went home. Seventeen hours later, I went to the hospital. Four surgeries and nine months later, I'm playing basketball again, but no kickball. I'm taking a break, no pun intended. For more of my adventures, check out my blog at *www.feistyflies. wordpress.com* and find me on Twitter *@DParker007*.

JENNY PURPLE is a writer, actor, comic, and improviser whose work has been seen coast to coast in New York, Los Angeles, Chicago, Austin, San Francisco, Santa Fe, South Carolina, and New Jersey on stage, screen, and television as well as internationally on the Internet and mobile devices distributed by Fun Little Movies. She has degrees in both acting and playwriting from Point Park University and Antioch University. Her political satire series can be seen at www.Bush TwinsPartyHour.com. Also an LGBT activist, Jenny was the face of www.noh8campaign.com/article/wear-purple-today-to-support-spiritday. Her triple award winning video *H8 of Love Game* can be seen on her YouTube channel Jenny Purple Productions. Follow her on Twitter *@jennypurple*.

BENJAMIN RIDGE is a writer, actor, comedian, and comedy producer based in London, England. In 2014 Benjamin achieved a masters in Drama and Theatre Studies, with a preprofessional year in Stand-up Comedy: First Class Honours, from the University of Kent, Canterbury, England. He spent 2013 studying in California as part of his degree and was warmly welcomed and enjoyed the world of improv comedy. He plans to move permanently to California in the near future so as to continue his work as an artist and creative being. At the end of 2015, Benjamin wrote, produced, and starred in a sellout production of *Box Clever*, at the Etcetera Theatre in Camden, London. As a young artist he is constantly looking to showcase his work and is delighted to be able to be included in this book. If you would like to read a smorgasbord of Benjamin's writing, check out his regularly updated blog at *https://benjaminridgeramblings. wordpress.com*.

ALESSANDRA RIZZOTTI is a demisexual panromantic*, who figured that out at age thirty while working as a communications manager at The Trevor Project, a suicide-prevention and crisis-intervention service for LGBTQ youth. Her pitch packets have helped writer Kirsten Smith (*Legally Blonde*, *10 Things I Hate About You*) sell two films to Paramount and ABC Family. She was featured on PRX reading from her Mortified journal and has written a poetry book titled *Homegrown*, as well as articles for *Hello Giggles*, *GOOD* magazine, The White House

---

*Has the potential to love all people, regardless of gender or sexuality, but doesn't feel sexual attraction unless emotionally connected.

blog, the United Nations, *Mend*, *Heeb*, *Backstage Magazine*, and four other monologue books for Hal Leonard/Applause in collaboration with Latin Grammy and Emmy Award–winner Alisha Gaddis. She beekeeps, occasionally edits children's chapbooks for 826 LA, and is currently working on a novel about finding her father. Find out more about her at *http://alessandrarizzotti.com* and follow her on Twitter *@hellorizzotti*.

JAMISON SCALA is an actor/comedian who is left-handed, redheaded, and gay. Help! Jamison is a graduate of The Second City Conservatory and performs regularly on its Hollywood stage. He has written and performed in videos including *Gay Ginger Breeders*, *Part of Your Office World—A Disney Parody*, *Coachella: What You Totes Need to Know*, and *Why You Shouldn't Mess with Redheads*. Raised in New Jersey (exit 145), he now calls Los Angeles home. His spirit animal is Judge Judy. You can follow his adventures at *JamisonScala.com* and *@MrJPScala*.

ILANA TURNER's first play, the award-winning *O Réjane*, premiered at Los Angeles's Bootleg Theater in November of 2014. *O Réjane* won the Stage Raw Los Angeles Theater Award for Female Leading Performance, and earned two additional nominations, including one for Ilana as playwright. Turner's one-act play, *In Her Voice*, is included in the 365 Women A Year playwriting project. Ilana previously worked as freelance writer for Turner Broadcasting and *Skater's Edge* magazine. As an actress on screen, Ilana has worked for HBO, Sci-Fi Channel, Spike TV, and has starred in the BAFTA/LA-nominated film

The Red Ace Cola Project. On stage, she starred in a world premiere at Edinburgh Fringe Festival and in Suzan-Lori Parks's *365 Plays for 365 Days*. Ilana holds a BA in theater and dance from Hampshire College. An ex-professional figure skater, she lives in Los Angeles with her husband and wee daughters. Find out more about her at *http://www.ilanaturner.com*.

KYLE T. WILSON is the author of over a dozen full-length plays, including *Yucca Corridor*; *Bumblefuck, AR*; and *The Butcher of Bumblebee*, among others. His play *After School Special* was a PlayLabs selection at the 2013 Great Plains Theatre Conference in Omaha, NE. Kyle is also executive producer of Los Angeles–based writer collective Fell Swoop Playwrights. He served as primary writer and producer of Fell Swoop's first two productions, *The Miss Julie Dream Project* and *The Last Temptation of Paula Deen*. *The Last Temptation of Paula Deen* premiered at the 2014 Hollywood Fringe Festival. *The Miss Julie Dream Project* premiered at the 2013 Hollywood Fringe and was remounted at Son of Semele Theater in September of that year. He has an MFA Carnegie Mellon University. Find out more about him at *http://fellswoopplaywrights.org/kyle-t-wilson*.

Acknowledgments

So many people to thank! I know I will not remember all of you. But I am grateful just the same. Xo Alisha

Thank you, Sara Camilli—you are extraordinary. You are my agent, but also my friend—what more could I ask for!

Thank you, writers. You guys did it! You created meaningful, funny work. Your words are powerful and will make change (and laughter!).

Thank you, Hal Leonard and Applause Books (especially John Cerullo and Marybeth Keating). Marybeth—through my pregnancy (aka the writing of this book), you have been nothing but kind and helpful. These six books in the series have been a delight and an honor because of you!

Thank you, Patty Hammond—copyeditor extraordinaire. You are the BEST! I mean it. You make the funny, funnier. Your eye is impeccable. Thanks for catching everything.

Thank you, Mom and Dad. You guys support it all—even if you have no idea what I am actually doing. (I don't usually know what I am doing!) I love you!

Thank you, Indiana Maven Diaz—my new baby. You make me want to make everything better. I want you to see your mother living a life of passion and art and going for her dreams! I want you to see failure and success in the artist life—and know that in the end, all that matters is that you created something you are proud of. You are the creation of which I am most proud. I love you, sweet baby girl.

Thank you, Lucky Diaz. Husband—you are more than words. I love you in the beginning and in the end. Thank you for your guidance and support. Thank you for understanding it all, even if you do not. Also, thank you for doing the electric slide in the delivery room with my mom. I love you the most.

And finally, thank you to all the LGBTQ community and its allies. I do not see this monologue book changing the world, but I see it opening doors for many. I hope somewhere in Indiana, a young middle school kid picks this book off the shelf and relates to everything. I hope a drag queen in the Lower East Side of Manhattan orders this book because she sees herself in one of the pieces. I hope a transgender college grad uses this book to audition for her first regional tour. I hope a straight ally delivers one of these monologues and represents her LGBTQ brothers and sisters. I hope you all believe in who you are—whoever that may be. Use these monologues, book the part, and set yourselves free!

More Titles from The Applause Acting Series

How I Did It
Establishing a Playwriting Career
edited by Lawrence Harbison
9781480369634................$24.99

25 10-Minute Plays for Teens
edited by Lawrence Harbison
9781480387768................$16.99

More 10-Minute Plays for Teens
edited by Lawrence Harbison
9781495011801................$9.99

10-Minute Plays for Kids
edited by Lawrence Harbison
9781495053399................$9.99

On Singing Onstage
by David Craig
9781557830432................$18.99

The Stanislavsky Technique: Russia
by Mel Gordon
9780936839080................$16.95

Speak with Distinction
by Edith Skinner/Revised with New Material Added by Timothy Monich and Lilene Mansell
9781557830470................$39.99

Recycling Shakespeare
by Charles Marowitz
9781557830944................$14.95

Acting in Film
by Michael Caine
9781557832771................$19.99

The Actor and the Text
by Cicely Berry
9781557831385................$22.99

The Craftsmen of Dionysus
by Jerome Rockwood
9781557831552................$19.99

A Performer Prepares
by David Craig
9781557833952................$19.99

Directing the Action
by Charles Marowitz
9781557830722................$18.99

Acting in Restoration Comedy
by Simon Callow
9781557831194................$18.99

Shakespeare's Plays in Performance
by John Russell Brown
9781557831361................$18.99

The Shakespeare Audition
How to Get Over Your Fear, Find the Right Piece, and Have a Great Audition
by Laura Wayth
9781495010804................$16.99

OTHER ACTING TITLES AVAILABLE

The Monologue Audition
A Practical Guide for Actors
by Karen Kohlhaas
9780879102913................$22.99

The Scene Study Book
Roadmap to Success
by Bruce Miller
9780879103712................$16.99

Acting Solo
Roadmap to Success
by Bruce Miller
9780879103750................$16.99

Actor's Alchemy
Finding the Gold in the Script
by Bruce Miller
9780879103835................$16.99

Stella Adler – The Art of Acting
compiled & edited by Howard Kissel
9781557833730................$29.99

Acting with Adler
by Joanna Rotté
9780879102982................$16.99

Accents
A Manual for Actors – Revised & Expanded Edition
by Robert Blumenfeld
9780879109677................$29.99

Acting with the Voice
The Art of Recording Books
by Robert Blumenfeld
9780879103019................$19.95

AN IMPRINT OF
HAL•LEONARD®
www.halleonardbooks.com

Prices, contents, and availability subject to change without notice.

1015

Monologue and Scene Books

**Best Contemporary
Monologues for Kids
Ages 7-15**
*edited by
Lawrence Harbison*
9781495011771 .... $16.99

**Best Contemporary
Monologues for Men
18-35**
*edited by
Lawrence Harbison*
9781480369610 .... $16.99

**Best Contemporary
Monologues for
Women 18-35**
*edited by
Lawrence Harbison*
9781480369627 .... $16.99

**Best Monologues
from The Best
American Short
Plays, Volume Three**
*edited by
William W. Demastes*
9781480397408 .... $19.99

**Best Monologues
from The Best
American Short
Plays, Volume Two**
*edited by
William W. Demastes*
9781480385481 .... $19.99

**Best Monologues
from The Best
American Short
Plays, Volume One**
*edited by
William W. Demastes*
9781480331556 .... $19.99

**The Best Scenes for
Kids Ages 7-15**
*edited by
Lawrence Harbison*
9781495011795 .... $16.99

Childsplay
A Collection of Scenes
and Monologues for
Children
edited by Kerry Muir
9780879101886 .... $16.99

**Duo!: The Best
Scenes for
Mature Actors**
edited by Stephen Fife
9781480360204 .... $19.99

**Duo!: The Best
Scenes for Two for
the 21st Century**
*edited by Joyce E. Henry,
Rebecca Dunn Jaroff, and
Bob Shuman*
9781557837028 .... $19.99

**Duo!: Best Scenes
for the 90's**
*edited by John Horvath,
Lavonne Mueller, and
Jack Temchin*
9781557830302 .... $18.99

**In Performance:
Contemporary
Monologues for Teens**
by JV Mercanti
9781480396616 .... $16.99

**In Performance:
Contemporary
Monologues for Men
and Women Late
Teens to Twenties**
by JV Mercanti
9781480331570 .... $18.99

**In Performance:
Contemporary
Monologues for
Men and Women
Late Twenties
to Thirties**
by JV Mercanti
9781480367470 .... $16.99

**Men's Comedic
Monologues That Are
Actually Funny**
edited by Alisha Gaddis
9781480396814 .... $14.99

**One on One: The Best
Men's Monologues
for the 21st Century**
*edited by Joyce E. Henry,
Rebecca Dunn Jaroff, and
Bob Shuman*
9781557837011 .... $18.99

**One on One: The Best
Women's Monologues
for the 21st Century**
*edited by Joyce E. Henry,
Rebecca Dunn Jaroff, and
Bob Shuman*
9781557837004 .... $18.99

**One on One: The Best
Men's Monologues
for the Nineties**
edited by Jack Temchin
9781557831514 .... $12.95

**One on One: The Best
Women's Monologues
for the Nineties**
edited by Jack Temchin
9781557831521 .... $11.95

**One on One: Playing
with a Purpose**
Monologues for Kids
Ages 7-15
*edited by Stephen Fife and
Bob Shuman with
contributing editors
Eloise Rollins-Fife and
Marit Shuman*
9781557838414 .... $16.99

**One on One: The
Best Monologues for
Mature Actors**
edited by Stephen Fife
9781480360198 .... $19.99

**Scenes and
Monologues
of Spiritual
Experience
from the Best
Contemporary Plays**
edited by Roger Ellis
9731480331563 .... $19.99

**Scenes and
Monologues from
Steinberg/ATCA New
Play Award Finalists,
2008-2012**
edited by Bruce Burgun
9781476868783 .... $19.99

Soliloquy!
The Shakespeare
Monologues
*edited by Michael Earley
and Philippa Keil*
9780936839783
Men's Edition $12.99
9780936839790
Women's Edition..... $14.95

**Teen Boys' Comedic
Monologues That Are
Actually Funny**
edited by Alisha Gaddis
9781480396791 .... $14.99

**Teens Girls' Comedic
Monologues That Are
Actually Funny**
edited by Alisha Gaddis
9781480396807 .... $14.99

**Women's Comedic
Monologues That Are
Actually Funny**
edited by Alisha Gaddis
9781480360426...... $14.99

AN IMPRINT OF

www.halleonardbooks.com